From Wallet to Wealth

From Wallet to Wealth

Beginner's guide to turning crypto basics into long-term value

Julien Ashcroft

Mindful Pages

Published in 2025

ISBN: 9789371770583 (PB)
ISBN: 9789371775489 (eBook)

Published by

Mindful Pages
Imprint of Alpha Editions LLC
312 W. 2nd St #1834
Casper, WY 82601, USA

This book was developed using advanced writing tools to support the drafting and ideation process. All content has been thoughtfully curated, refined, and reviewed to ensure quality and relevance.

Content

Introduction
Rethinking Wealth in a Programmable Age

What if the real force behind cryptocurrency had little to do with charts or price swings—and everything to do with how we see the world?

For more than a decade, the public conversation has latched on to the spectacle: Bitcoin's wild surges, the implosions of strange-sounding tokens, maverick billionaires, and audacious traders. It's a narrative built on fascination laced with fear. Yet, if you tune out the noise—push past the hype cycles and tribal loyalties—there's a quieter, deeper current. That's where this book begins. Not with instructions on opening a wallet or decoding blockchain jargon, but with a shift in perspective: cryptocurrency is more than a financial tool. It's a threshold in thinking. A mirror held up to culture. And, most of all, a test.

A test of whether you can keep your head when the world is shouting.
A test of how you define value in an era where numbers seem to mean less than they once did.
A test of whether you can act with conviction when no outcome is guaranteed.

This is, technically, a beginner's guide—but not in the way you might expect. It doesn't assume you're here to hunt for the next "buy the dip" opportunity or master the alphabet soup of crypto slang. You won't find repackaged investment tips or the lure of overnight wealth. Instead, *From Wallet to Wealth* offers something rarer: an invitation to slow down, think harder, and ask sharper questions. To reconsider what it truly means to build wealth—not just in digital terms, but in personal, philosophical, and even generational ones.

We now inhabit what could rightly be called a programmable economy—one where markets operate without pause, across every timezone, guided not by the decrees of a boardroom but by code itself. In this space, "decentralisation" is no empty slogan; it's a design for a different kind of agency. But the real upheaval lies not in the technology—it's in what the technology exposes about us.

The greatest shift crypto brings is mental, not monetary. It forces us to re-examine old questions: What is trust? What does it mean to own something? How does anything gain value in the first place? And in posing these questions, it draws attention to how often we've allowed institutions, governments, and experts to answer them on our behalf. In the decentralised, self-directed world crypto promises, those questions come back to you.

This return of responsibility can be exhilarating—or terrifying. Without middlemen, there's no one left to blame. If you hold the keys, you also hold the risk. There's no central bank to rescue you, no customer service line to reverse your misstep. In this landscape, wealth is no longer a matter of accumulation alone—it's shaped by clarity, discipline, and the resilience to stand firm amid uncertainty.

And so this book starts from a philosophical footing: your wealth isn't measured by what your digital wallet displays, but by how you define value, how you choose when the ground is shifting, and how you guard your beliefs in a marketplace ruled by stories. Before crypto can alter your finances, it must sharpen your mind.

Money, before it was a system, was always a story. We like to imagine it as a hard science—precise, objective, indifferent. History tells otherwise. The earliest forms of currency were shells, beads, notched sticks, carved bones—objects with no intrinsic worth, but imbued with meaning through shared belief. Trust was the true infrastructure; money was merely its interface.

In that sense, Bitcoin is not a break from tradition but its digital heir—familiar in essence, radical in reach. It is borderless, permissionless, programmable. Its boldest act is not in existing, but in redistributing the power to shape value itself—a role once monopolised by monarchs, banks, and empires. Anyone can now opt into a new consensus—or step away from it entirely.

This openness makes the matter deeply personal. Without institutions to set the standard, the responsibility for deciding what is valuable shifts inward. Each choice—whether to invest, hold, or exit—becomes a small act of self-definition. What, exactly, are you betting on? A whitepaper's promises? A token's trajectory? Or your own ability to think and act with clarity?

This is not a book that glorifies crypto, nor one that dismisses it as a passing mania. Instead, it places crypto where it belongs—at the junction of culture, economics, and psychology. The market's volatility doesn't merely reflect price—it reflects us: our ambitions, our anxieties, our craving for meaning in a digital age.

Yes, the landscape is littered with frauds and distractions. But it also hums with genuine signal. Beneath the surface chaos, a new infrastructure is taking shape—reshaping how we transact, coordinate, and form belonging. Decentralised protocols. Tokenised communities. Programmable ownership. These are not just technical features; they are provocations. They raise unsettling questions: What happens when finance becomes culture? When identity becomes data? When a joke—a meme—can sway a market?

Such questions are not reserved for coders or traders. They matter to anyone who senses that the old economic order is straining, and that something unformed—but potent—is rising in its place.

This book is designed to help you navigate that liminal space.

Chapter One strips money down to its roots, treating it as a social contract and showing how crypto, rather than being a wholly new invention, resurrects first principles. Chapter Two turns inward, mapping the emotional and psychological groundwork of belief—how to develop conviction before committing capital, and how to cultivate the long-term mindset that can survive a culture addicted to immediacy.

By Chapter Three, we dig beneath coin prices to uncover the layered architecture of the crypto ecosystem—protocols, communities, networks—and learn how to evaluate them as living digital economies rather than mere financial instruments.

Chapter Four shifts to the social sphere, exploring how crypto's technology also fosters belonging—and the risks that come with forming identity inside digital tribes.

Chapter Five tackles volatility not simply as financial turbulence, but as an emotional crucible. It offers ways to read market storms as mirrors of our own attachments and insecurities, and tools to navigate them with steadiness and self-awareness.

In Chapter Six, self-custody becomes both a practical and philosophical concern. We examine what it means to truly own your assets—and, by extension, your choices—while considering how digital wallets may soon hold far more than currency.

Chapter Seven widens the lens, arguing that crypto is less a fleeting trend than a generational inflection point. Here, we confront the impatience of "getting rich quick" with an alternative: building an ethos of stewardship and legacy.

Chapter Eight turns to practice—constructing the habits, systems, and safeguards that help you participate in crypto with clarity and discipline.

Chapter Nine steps into moral terrain. In a permissionless world, what anchors right and wrong? We explore the grey areas, the temptations, and the chance to practise a form of ethical capitalism suited to decentralisation.

Finally, Chapter Ten circles back to you. When the numbers evaporate, what remains? What wealth endures off-chain—in character, in choices, in clarity?

This book isn't written for the early adopter seeking a pat on the back, nor for the opportunist chasing the next pump. It's written for those who see that the real challenge of crypto isn't playing the game, but holding your integrity as the rules keep changing.

From Wallet to Wealth is a guide for navigating complexity with both curiosity and conscience. For those prepared to ask not just, "What is this worth?" but, "What am I becoming in the process?"

You may arrive for crypto. You'll leave with something greater.

Chapter 1
The Myth of Money – Why Crypto Isn't the Revolution You Think It Is

Every upheaval worth the name begins not with a shiny new invention, but with a challenge to a long-entrenched belief. Cryptocurrency is often painted in the popular imagination as a kind of financial insurgency—an upstart movement storming the citadels of Wall Street, rattling the presses of central banks, and threatening the monopolies of legacy institutions. It is a dramatic story, and an alluring one. Yet it misses something more subversive at work. Crypto is not merely ushering in a novel asset class or a quicker way to move funds. It is, at its core, compelling us to re-examine the very idea of money—its nature, its mechanisms, and the strange, stubborn reasons we trust it. To grasp what crypto might become, we must first confront the myth it dares to disturb.

The word *money* carries a false clarity. We think we know it: what we earn, what we spend, what we tuck away for later. It seems solid enough—pounds, euros, dollars; crisp notes, digital figures, the comforting certainty of a price label in a shop window. But this familiarity conceals a deeper, older truth. Money is, and has always been, a shared story—part social pact, part illusion, kept alive by our collective faith. It is not a product of nature, nor the inevitable outcome of scientific necessity. Rather, it is a cultural fiction reinforced by ritual and steeped in centuries of power, identity, and aspiration.

That money rests on narrative rather than objective substance is hardly a novel thought, yet it remains persistently underestimated. Take the pound sterling. It once signified an actual pound of silver. Today, it signifies a claim backed only by faith in the issuing state. The paper note in your wallet is intrinsically worthless; its value comes from your readiness to accept it—and from the unspoken certainty that others will as well. This suspension of disbelief enables a central bank to "inject liquidity," a government to "raise the debt ceiling," or a market to "rally on confidence." These are not immutable laws of physics. They are performances of consensus.

When Satoshi Nakamoto released the Bitcoin white paper in 2008, he was not unveiling a new form of money in the scientific sense. He was offering a fresh mythology—one grounded not in sovereign authority or gold reserves, but in mathematics, transparency, and personal sovereignty. Like all mythologies, it came complete with symbols (₿), rituals (mining, halving), and its own priesthood (core developers, maximalists, influencers). To the casual observer, Bitcoin might look like a digital asset; to anyone reading the cultural subtext, it is a belief system. The ledger may be decentralised, but its meaning is deeply human.

The first rupture crypto brings, then, is not to banks or payment rails, but to the illusion that money is objective. It reminds us—bluntly—that even the most venerable currencies rest on shared stories. Some tales are ancient, others fresh, but all are open to revision. Bitcoin did not replace fiat; it exposed its fragility. It made plain what had always been tacit: money is an exercise in belief management. In doing so, it created a market not just for tokens, but for the stories those tokens carry.

If that sounds lofty, consider how markets actually behave. Investors shift billions based on a central banker's phrasing; prices rise or fall because consumers *feel* optimistic or anxious; a meme sends a coin's value into the stratosphere. What is changing hands here? Not raw fundamentals. Not cold data. But belief, expectation, mood. Money, far from being a neutral tool, is a theatre of human psychology. Crypto did not create this theatre—it simply tore down the curtains so we could see the stage.

From here, the second disruption follows naturally: authority. Much ink has been spilled on how cryptocurrencies circumvent traditional intermediaries. They do not require a central bank to issue them, a commercial bank to process them, or a government to decree their legitimacy. Yet the deeper challenge lies in what this decentralisation says about control itself. For centuries, money has been the medium through which authority asserts itself. To issue currency is to wield dominion; to control its value is to shape reality. When Rome struck coins bearing the emperor's profile, it was proclaiming sovereignty as much as facilitating trade. When colonial powers imposed their currencies abroad, they were scripting obedience into economic life.

Crypto, in contrast, suggests an entirely different posture. It does not call for rebellion; it offers the option to walk away. No coups, no barricades—just the quiet possibility of opting out. In doing so, it decentralises legitimacy itself. You need not plead with a sovereign to mint your money. You need not be born within a regime to gain access to its financial tools. You need not inherit the defaults of your economic identity. You can choose. And that act of choosing is, in its own understated way, revolutionary.

Such freedom, however, can be dizzying. Authority, for all its imperfections, gives us a framework—a ready-made set of rules to follow or resist. Without it, responsibility falls squarely on the individual. The notorious volatility of crypto markets is partly the manifestation of this psychological disorientation. Without central arbiters to steady expectations, belief is more brittle, more prone to sudden turns. Values swing not solely on supply and demand, but on our collective attempt to define, in real time, what value even means. It is not the market alone that is unstable—it is our shared sense of certainty still finding its footing.

And the implications extend beyond finance. Holding crypto is not just about possessing an asset; it is about signalling a worldview—one that prizes decentralisation, code as law, and autonomy over imposed authority. The language of early adopters—sovereignty, censorship resistance, "escaping the system"—is not mere technical description. It is existential. Crypto becomes a stage for self-definition, much as money always has.

To trace the lineage is to see the arc of currency evolve: from the Lydians' stamped coins to medieval rulers' debasement schemes, from the colonial imposition of currency to crypto's programmable code. Each change in form reshaped how people understood themselves, their rulers, and their place in the world. With crypto, the unit of value is not merely minted—it is coded. Transactions become logic, and belief itself begins to feel programmable.

Thus the cultural dimension of crypto cannot be ignored. A blockchain is more than a ledger—it is a medium for experimenting with new social contracts. Ethereum, for instance, is not just a platform for tokens; it is a programmable economy, a system for governance, coordination, and exchange. To use it is to take part in building an evolving framework of meaning and value. The lexicon—gas fees, DAOs, layer-2s, tokenomics—may sound forbidding, but it encodes genuine innovations in how value is created, shared, and understood. Value here is not fixed; it is emergent, relational, a co-creation of the community that sustains it. This is no passing financial fad—it is a shift in the sociology of value itself.

Yet because it operates on many layers at once, crypto is easy to misread. To some, it is little more than speculative frenzy; to others, a feat of engineering; to yet others, a philosophical provocation about trust and meaning. Each lens offers a fragment of the truth, but only together do they reveal its full reach. Crypto is not the revolution most assume—not because it falls short, but because it aims wider. It is not simply a backlash against centralised finance; it is a reframing of how we believe, how we organise, how we decide what is worth what.

Which is why the myth of money is not a detour but the entrance. Long before you acquire a token, you are participating in a belief system. Before you open a digital wallet, you are immersed in stories about value, power, and legitimacy. To navigate this terrain honestly, you must learn to see these stories—how they are built, how they shape behaviour, and how they exert their quiet force.

This chapter will take you there: back to money's roots, through the myths that underlie even the most 'rational' of systems, and into the tensions between power and trust that crypto revives. It will not hand you tidy answers, but it will leave you with sharper questions. And in an age where code can shape currency, those questions may well be the most valuable asset you hold.

The Origins of Trust

Before money was minted, before banks were founded, before anything resembling a market economy existed, human beings were already exchanging value. Not through coins or notes, but through trust—intangible, often unspoken, yet vital. Long before any economy could be formalised, it had to be imagined. And what makes an economy imaginable is not metal, or mathematics, or markets. It's belief. That you'll honour a debt. That I'll accept your offering. That something intangible today might hold value tomorrow. Trust, not currency, is the foundational currency of civilisation.

This is not poetic exaggeration. Anthropological evidence tells us that early humans—long before agricultural surpluses or city-states—engaged in reciprocal exchange systems rooted in social obligation and memory. In small groups, value flowed through webs of shared reputation. A hunter would share meat with others not for immediate compensation, but with the implicit expectation that the favour would be returned. These exchanges were not transactional in the modern sense. They were trust-based, enforced by the relational gravity of community. To break trust was to risk exclusion—a punishment often harsher than any fine.

Such systems persisted for millennia, and indeed, in many parts of the world, they still do. Gift economies, informal credit arrangements, and community lending circles operate outside of formal finance but rely on something older and arguably more resilient: social capital. These systems demonstrate that the architecture of value does not begin with state-issued currency. It begins with memory, obligation, and mutual dependence.

When money eventually emerged, it did not replace trust—it codified it. The first coins, minted in Lydia around 600 BCE, were stamped with the images of rulers to guarantee weight and purity. But the real guarantee was psychological: a shared belief that these objects represented something more than metal. That belief wasn't generated by the coins themselves, but by the authority that backed them. It was the reputation of the issuer—the sovereign, the temple, the state—that made the currency trustworthy.

The act of minting was, fundamentally, an act of narrative. It told the user: "You can rely on this." But behind that promise lay a series of preconditions: political stability, social cohesion, and a degree of collective memory that could tie this object in your hand to an expected future. Currency was, in essence, portable trust. It allowed strangers to transact without knowing each other because they both believed in the underlying guarantor. It abstracted relationships and scaled cooperation—but the emotional and cognitive foundations remained the same.

This is why the rise of fiat currency represented such a pivotal psychological shift. Fiat—by definition—derives its value not from intrinsic worth but from state decree. "Fiat" means "let it be done." Its authority is not in its substance, but in its story. When we accept it, we are not trusting the paper—we are trusting the institutional scaffolding behind it. The courts that enforce contracts. The central banks that manage inflation. The governments that collect taxes in that currency. This is often mistaken as a technical arrangement, but it is profoundly cultural. To accept fiat is to subscribe to a nation's narrative of order, legitimacy, and future solvency.

And this is precisely what cryptocurrency upends—not because it removes trust, but because it reassigns it. Crypto doesn't eliminate belief; it relocates it from institutions to protocols. From governments to code. From historical authority to computational transparency. Bitcoin, for instance, offers no interest rate, no centralised issuer, and no backing in the traditional sense. Its legitimacy is mathematical, not institutional. What we're trusting is the protocol's integrity, the distributed consensus, the immutability of a ledger maintained not by decree but by cryptographic proof.

This is a return, not an invention. It echoes the pre-monetary trust systems that relied on memory and reciprocity—only now, that memory is encoded across a global network, and the reciprocity is enforced by open-source logic rather than social obligation. Crypto reframes trust as something that can be distributed and automated, rather than centralised and mediated. It doesn't discard the human need for belief; it just rewires the mechanism.

Consider the shift from promissory notes issued by goldsmiths—effectively early banks—to smart contracts on Ethereum. Both serve the same function: to formalise a promise. But while the former depended on the perceived solvency of the issuer, the latter depends on the transparency and predictability of the code. In both cases, we are dealing with trust—but in very different registers. One is anchored in reputation and social authority; the other in auditability and decentralised execution. Both, however, are stories we tell to make risk acceptable.

And this is where the tension lies. The modern state has long monopolised the machinery of monetary trust. Central banks manage inflation expectations through forward guidance; financial institutions enforce creditworthiness via opaque scoring systems. These systems are designed to produce stability, but they also demand a kind of passive compliance. The average citizen is not invited to interrogate how money works—only to use it. Crypto disrupts this passivity by making the architecture of trust visible and, in some cases, negotiable. To engage with blockchain-based finance is to be pulled into an explicit confrontation with the machinery of belief.

This confrontation is not just technical. It is emotional. Because trust, in human psychology, is not a binary. It is layered, experiential, and deeply contextual. We trust people, institutions, and systems for different reasons, and those reasons often conflict. You may trust a government-issued currency because you believe in the rule of law, even as you distrust its fiscal policy. You may trust Bitcoin's scarcity model while doubting the security of a particular exchange. Crypto does not resolve these tensions—it surfaces them. And in doing so, it asks something more demanding from its users: self-responsibility.

When you custody your own assets, there is no customer service line. When you send a transaction, there is no undo button. These conditions create a different kind of trust—less about assurance, more about awareness. You are not trusting a third party to protect you. You are trusting yourself to understand the risks. This is exhilarating for some, paralysing for others. But in both cases, it marks a return to a more primitive, and arguably more honest, conception of trust: not as outsourced certainty, but as negotiated agency.

This reintroduction of responsibility has philosophical implications. It challenges the assumption that trust must always be delegated upwards—to banks, governments, platforms. It suggests that trust can be a bottom-up phenomenon, coordinated through consensus and encoded into shared systems. And it implies that belief, far from being irrational or sentimental, is the very substrate upon which economies are built.

The irony is that many critics of crypto view it as a solution in search of a problem, accusing it of inventing complexity where none is needed. But that critique fails to recognise that our existing monetary systems are themselves deeply complex—just comfortably so. They are layered with assumptions, history, and inherited architectures that most users never need to examine. Crypto doesn't add complexity; it reveals it. It turns the black box of money inside out and asks: what do you *actually* trust?

This question is not limited to finance. It applies equally to media, governance, science, and social order. Trust has become the contested resource of the 21st century. We live in an age where institutional confidence is eroding, information is decentralised, and authority is increasingly subject to peer review and public scrutiny. Crypto is not an outlier in this landscape—it is a reflection of it. It is a test case for a broader cultural experiment: can systems built on distributed trust outperform those built on inherited authority?

There is no definitive answer yet. The crypto ecosystem remains volatile, uneven, and in some cases, exploitative. But its very existence challenges us to reconsider what trust *means*—how it's built, where it resides, and who gets to define it. In this way, crypto doesn't represent a clean break from monetary history. It is its next chapter. A continuation of humanity's long-standing effort to formalise cooperation, reduce friction, and manage uncertainty—not through magic, but through meaning.

What began as oral promises in tribal camps evolved into tokens, ledgers, and monetary policy. Now, it continues as consensus algorithms and smart contracts. The tools change, but the substrate remains the same. Trust is not a by-product of money. It is its precondition. And in that sense, cryptocurrency is not a futuristic innovation. It is an ancient idea—reborn in code.

Money as Story, Not Science

If money were purely rational, it would not be this powerful. It would be a neutral medium—a passive facilitator of exchange governed by arithmetic, held in balance by market forces, and stripped of drama. But money is not neutral. It is never just numbers on a spreadsheet or coins in a pocket. It is narrative. And like any good story, it thrives on belief, fear, hope, and collective imagination. To mistake it for science is to misread its function entirely.

At its core, money is a shared fiction—an agreement about value that only exists because we act as if it does. This is not to say that money is unreal, but rather that its reality is performative. It is created not through intrinsic worth, but through sustained belief. You accept payment in a currency because you trust that someone else will too. That expectation is not enforced by logic; it is maintained by participation. Its power lies not in its composition, but in its narrative strength.

Consider the dollar. It is the world's dominant reserve currency, yet it is backed by no physical commodity. Its value is propped up by faith in the United States government and its financial institutions, underwritten by a legal system, a tax regime, a military presence, and a global consensus. None of these are equations. They are trust architectures, mythologies formalised through legal tender laws and central bank policy. What you are holding when you hold a dollar is not a unit of fixed value—it is a claim on a story. A story that says: this will be worth something tomorrow because others believe it will be.

This same dynamic applies across economic systems. The euro exists because a group of sovereign nations decided to subordinate monetary independence to a collective fiction of continental integration. The Japanese yen functions on the back of internal economic cohesion, not external demand for its paper. Even highly inflationary currencies like the Zimbabwean dollar or Venezuelan bolívar persist beyond rational thresholds of utility because belief—however fragile—takes time to die. People continue to transact, not because it makes sense, but because it's what they know. *Belief resists disruption, even when the facts collapse beneath it.*

This belief-centred view of money is not just philosophical—it is observable. Stock market movements often diverge from fundamentals and instead respond to sentiment, narrative shifts, or geopolitical mood swings. Asset bubbles form not due to sudden changes in value, but because belief outruns substance. Tulip mania in 17th-century Holland. The dot-com boom of the late 1990s. Meme stocks in 2021. These episodes are not aberrations—they are clarifying episodes that reveal the behavioural undercurrent that money flows on.

The role of narrative becomes even more explicit in marketing and brand strategy, where value is manufactured through story. A handbag, a sneaker, or a watch may be technically unremarkable, yet its price can soar due to the brand mythology surrounding it. Money, in this sense, is not only a tool for pricing stories—it is itself a story that shapes how we understand what is valuable. And when that story shifts, markets move.

Bitcoin understood this earlier than its critics did. From the beginning, it was marketed not just as a digital currency, but as a rebellion. Its pseudonymous creator, Satoshi Nakamoto, embedded a critique of central banking in the genesis block: *"The Times 03/Jan/2009 Chancellor on brink of second bailout for banks."* This was not a technical statement. It was a narrative signal. It positioned Bitcoin as a response to systemic failure and moral hazard—a currency uncorrupted by institutional discretion. The code may have been elegant, but it was the story that made it viral.

And stories spread not because they are true, but because they are *believable*. Bitcoin's scarcity model—capped at 21 million coins—mimics gold in a way that evokes intuitive trust. It says, "this cannot be inflated, therefore it is safe." Ethereum, meanwhile, tells a different story: not of money, but of programmable coordination. It invites users to imagine an open-source financial system, where smart contracts replace middlemen. Both narratives tap into dissatisfaction with the existing financial order—but they do so with different aesthetics, different heroes, and different visions of the future. These are not just technologies. They are myth-making machines.

The power of myth should not be confused with deception. Myth does not mean falsehood. It means meaning. A myth is a culturally encoded framework for understanding how the world works and what matters. It can be sacred, secular, ancient, or new. Money, like religion or law, gains force not through empirical verification but through collective enactment. It works because we behave as though it does. This is why monetary systems must be understood sociologically, not just economically. They are expressions of belief systems, embedded in culture, identity, and power.

Take the global dominance of the U.S. dollar. It is not a function of its physical characteristics, but of the story it tells: America as stable, strong, and solvent. As long as that story holds, the dollar holds. But stories are fragile. They can be eroded by geopolitical missteps, internal political dysfunction, or better narratives emerging elsewhere. If the world believes that an alternative system—whether yuan-based, crypto-native, or otherwise—offers a more credible story of value and continuity, it will begin to shift. Not because of charts, but because of conviction.

This insight complicates the common view of cryptocurrencies as simply high-tech finance. To participate in crypto is to choose a new story—to buy into a different myth of what money is and who should control it. Whether one aligns with Bitcoin's scarcity narrative, Ethereum's utility proposition, or Solana's speed-first gospel, the decision is not purely rational. It is *theological in structure*, if not in content. There is a leap of faith. There are high priests. There are schisms and sects. Each chain carries its own cultural logic, its own language of legitimacy. Understanding these dynamics is essential not just for investors, but for anyone trying to make sense of where value is going.

Critics of crypto often point to volatility as evidence of its unfitness. But volatility is the natural condition of any narrative under construction. Unlike fiat, which is stabilised through decades of habituated belief and institutional reinforcement, crypto is still negotiating its meaning. Its value is not unstable because it lacks fundamentals; it is unstable because its story is still being written. The volatility reflects not technical weakness, but interpretive flux. Markets aren't just deciding what crypto is worth—they are still deciding what it *is*.

And that is why framing money as story rather than science is crucial. It allows us to approach financial systems not as immutable facts, but as changeable structures of meaning. This doesn't mean abandoning rational analysis, but it does mean supplementing it with cultural literacy. Why do people believe in this currency and not that one? What social, historical, or psychological forces support or erode that belief? What moral frameworks are embedded in its use or rejection? These are not marginal questions. They are central to understanding both the resilience and fragility of monetary regimes.

As crypto matures, the battleground will not be technical specifications or transaction speeds alone—it will be narrative superiority. Which protocol tells the most compelling, coherent, and credible story about value, governance, and identity? Which ecosystem generates the trust, imagination, and commitment of its users? In short, which myth wins? The protocols with the best stories will survive not because they are more efficient, but because they better capture the collective mind.

None of this renders money irrational or delusional. On the contrary, it affirms its deep rationality as a social technology. But that rationality operates within a framework of belief, not detached from it. Money works because we agree it works. And our reasons for agreement are as varied as our histories, cultures, and aspirations. Understanding that is not optional—it is essential.

To see money as a story is not to devalue it, but to understand its value more clearly. It is to recognise that belief is not a flaw in financial systems, but their very foundation. And in that recognition, we begin to see why crypto matters—not as a replacement for the old story, but as a challenge to its monopoly. Not because it tells the only truth, but because it dares to tell a new one.

What Crypto Really Disrupts

If you believe cryptocurrency's primary threat lies in its potential to unseat the banking industry, you are looking too narrowly. Crypto does indeed bypass intermediaries, displace traditional payment systems, and decentralise financial infrastructure. But these are surface effects—consequences, not causes. The real disruption posed by crypto runs deeper. It challenges not merely systems of exchange, but the structures of authority, the logic of institutional control, and even the psychological frameworks through which individuals derive identity and self-worth. It is less a financial revolution than a reconfiguration of power—economic, political, and personal.

To begin understanding the magnitude of this disruption, consider what modern institutions actually do. Banks, governments, and regulatory bodies do not merely hold money or enforce rules. They monopolise trust. They mediate legitimacy. They decide what is "real," what counts as ownership, and whose interpretation of value is enforceable. When a state issues currency, it does more than print notes—it declares its sovereignty over economic imagination. Crypto, in contrast, does not just create new tools. It introduces a different mental architecture. It invites participants to question why authority must flow from above, why trust must be imposed rather than chosen, and why economic identity should be inherited rather than designed.

What crypto disrupts, then, is not the mechanics of finance but its metaphysics. It takes aim at the belief—so deeply ingrained as to be invisible—that control is something properly centralised, decisions are best made from the top, and financial power must always be mediated by third parties. Bitcoin did not just remove banks from the equation; it removed the assumption that banks, or any central authority, were necessary to begin with. It dared to ask: what if consensus could be engineered without permission?

This is not a technical question. It is philosophical. It reshapes the social contract, reducing dependence on institutional validation and placing responsibility directly into the hands of the user. Such a shift can be exhilarating for those ready to accept it, and terrifying for those who are not. After all, institutions offer more than services—they offer psychological shelter. They provide frameworks for decision-making, buffers against uncertainty, and clear lines of accountability. Crypto, by contrast, demands a radical form of self-authorship. To participate fully is to step into a system where you are not only the beneficiary, but the guarantor. There is no one to call if your wallet is hacked, no central bank to stabilise your assets, no regulator to rewind your mistakes. The promise of empowerment is inseparable from the demand for autonomy.

This is why, beyond institutions, crypto disrupts individuals. It undermines conventional markers of identity, status, and success. In traditional finance, wealth accumulation often reflects conformity—climbing hierarchical structures, aligning with institutional norms, navigating regulatory systems. In crypto, wealth is increasingly linked to early insight, unconventional thinking, and ideological conviction. Someone who understood the implications of Ethereum in 2016, or who contributed to a nascent decentralised protocol before it was fashionable, may now wield enormous economic power—outside of any traditional credentialing system. This inversion of prestige is unsettling to elites whose influence depends on gatekeeping. But it is not an accident. It is a consequence of decentralised networks valuing contribution over permission, creativity over credential.

And this recalibration extends to authority more broadly. Crypto erodes the monopoly that nation-states have long held over value and verification. It allows for the emergence of self-sovereign identity—where individuals can prove attributes, ownership, or legitimacy without reliance on a government-issued ID. Consider the implications: if your economic reputation lives on-chain, portable and verifiable, you are no longer tethered to the bureaucratic frameworks of a single nation. You become, in a sense, economically stateless. This is not science fiction. It is already unfolding through decentralised identity protocols, NFT-based credentialing systems, and on-chain social graphs. These tools don't just change how you interact with the economy—they change how you define yourself within it.

The reaction from existing power structures is telling. Regulatory scrutiny of crypto is not solely about consumer protection or systemic risk. It is about narrative control. When governments express concern over decentralised finance, what they are often reacting to is not the technology's volatility, but its autonomy. It operates outside the bounds of fiscal policy, monetary issuance, and traditional compliance regimes. It poses uncomfortable questions: What happens when people stop needing central banks? What if trust becomes programmable? What if economic coordination can emerge without law? These are not hypotheticals. They are live challenges to the epistemological foundations of modern governance.

This also helps explain why the disruption is not evenly distributed. Crypto doesn't threaten Wall Street in the way many assume. Financial institutions are, by design, adaptable. They are already finding ways to co-opt the tools of crypto—offering custody services, launching crypto ETFs, integrating blockchain for settlements. The logic of capital is flexible: if value flows into new channels, legacy actors will follow. In many cases, they already are. What is far more deeply threatened is the worldview that made those actors necessary in the first place. *Crypto disrupts not markets, but mentalities.*

At the personal level, this disruption often expresses itself in an existential re-evaluation of agency. In a decentralised system, there is no one to blame for poor decisions, no external authority to validate your strategies, no fallback when belief falters. This can induce clarity or crisis, depending on one's psychological readiness. For some, it becomes a forge for conviction—an opportunity to craft a personal investment thesis, to build frameworks for evaluating risk, to own mistakes and learn from them without institutional hand-holding. For others, it reveals how deeply they have relied on external structures for stability and direction. Crypto becomes not just a market, but a mirror—showing you what you actually believe about responsibility, risk, and reward.

This is also why community becomes so central. Without traditional institutions to mediate trust, people form their own. Telegram groups, Discord servers, DAOs—these are the new centres of coordination and belief. But unlike corporate boards or centralised bureaucracies, they are often chaotic, experimental, and emotionally charged. They rely on social norms, shared memes, and tokenised incentives to function. These emergent communities are not a sideshow—they are the operating system of the new order. And in them, we see a preview of how legitimacy might evolve: less imposed, more emergent; less formal, more cultural.

Yet even as crypto fragments authority and challenges institutional power, it does not eliminate the human need for structure. It replaces formal hierarchy with networked influence. Influencers, developers, community leaders—they gain prominence not through appointment, but through attention. The social capital of crypto is volatile, and reputation is both decentralised and hyper-visible. This produces new dynamics: accountability is enforced not by title, but by transparency. When every wallet, governance vote, and transaction is publicly inspectable, credibility becomes performative. This can lead to toxicity or innovation, depending on how systems are designed—but either way, the old safeguards no longer apply.

None of this guarantees a utopia. Decentralisation is not inherently virtuous. It can empower innovation or chaos. It can dissolve harmful monopolies or fuel new forms of exploitation. But what it *does* do—unmistakably—is redistribute the locus of power. It demands that we stop asking who is in charge, and start asking how decisions are made. It forces a reorientation of authority away from inherited legitimacy and toward provable contribution. And it challenges every individual to rethink what it means to have control—over money, identity, and meaning.

This is what crypto really disrupts: the consensus about where power should reside, who gets to speak, and what makes something worth believing in. It is not a clean replacement of banks or a bypass of fiat. It is a systemic interrogation of authority—one that reaches far beyond finance. When you hold a private key, when you join a DAO, when you sign a transaction on a permissionless network, you are not just using a new tool. You are engaging in a new politics. One where control is no longer conferred by hierarchy, but composed through choice. And that shift—subtle, uncomfortable, often invisible—is the true revolution.

From Coins to Codes: A Cultural Leap

Every monetary system is a mirror. It reflects not only what a society values, but how it sees itself—its myths, its power structures, its aspirations, and its sense of order. Coins, colonial currencies, and cryptographic ledgers may seem like disparate forms of economic technology, but each represents a distinct stage in the cultural evolution of identity and authority. To understand where crypto fits in this lineage, and what it truly disrupts, we must begin by acknowledging an often-overlooked truth: money is never just a medium of exchange. It is also a medium of meaning.

The earliest coins minted by the Lydians around the 7th century BCE were not designed merely to facilitate trade. They were instruments of political legitimacy. Embossed with the image of a sovereign or a divine symbol, they did more than assure weight or purity—they communicated trust, hierarchy, and allegiance. The moment a ruler's face appeared on a coin, the medium stopped being neutral. It became a tool of propaganda. To use that coin was to participate in a shared recognition of the issuer's authority. The image legitimised the value, and the coin, in turn, legitimised the regime. Currency became a form of soft control, embedding identity into daily economic life.

This entanglement of money and identity only deepened with empire. Under Roman rule, the spread of currency was as much a cultural project as a logistical one. Roman coins were distributed across provinces bearing Latin inscriptions and imperial portraits—

asserting not only the reach of the empire, but its ideological supremacy. Later, European colonial powers perfected this model. In India, Africa, Southeast Asia, and the Caribbean, colonial currencies were introduced not simply to ease trade, but to supplant indigenous value systems. The introduction of the rupee, the franc, or the pound in colonised regions did more than displace barter—it dislocated identity. Traditional systems of exchange, which had often been embedded in kinship, ritual, or local trust networks, were replaced by the abstract authority of foreign empires. The currency imposed was a psychological directive: to participate in the colonial economy, you had to convert—not just your resources, but your worldview.

These examples reveal a consistent pattern: control over currency is also control over narrative. Money functions as an inscription of legitimacy—who gets to assign value, who governs trade, who defines the centre and who exists at the periphery. It is no accident that nation-states still consider monetary sovereignty sacred. Control over currency issuance is control over the national story. This is why hyperinflation, as seen in Zimbabwe or Weimar Germany, is not just a financial crisis—it is a crisis of identity. When a currency collapses, the story it upheld collapses with it. People are left not just poorer, but disoriented.

This brings us to the cultural leap crypto represents. It does not merely offer a new monetary instrument; it offers a new way of writing the script itself. For the first time in history, value can be created, transacted, and secured without any central authority. No sovereign face, no imperial mandate, no national bank. Instead, value is governed by open-source protocols, cryptographic consensus, and voluntary participation. This decentralised infrastructure challenges the centuries-old idea that identity must be shaped by geography or institutions. It suggests that identity can now be self-authored, portable, and anchored in code.

The cultural implications are profound. Take the emergence of Ethereum-based social tokens or DAOs (Decentralised Autonomous Organisations). These are not just financial tools; they are vehicles for community identity. A DAO is, in effect, a programmable tribe—defined not by geography, bloodline, or bureaucracy, but by shared purpose and mutual stakeholding. Its members coordinate using tokens, vote using smart contracts, and define membership criteria autonomously. Value here is not imposed top-down; it is negotiated laterally, iteratively, and often messily. Yet this messiness is precisely what makes it democratic. It reflects the social texture of human cooperation without requiring the apparatus of the state.

Consider also the phenomenon of non-fungible tokens (NFTs). Much of the public discourse around NFTs has been trivialised by media portrayals focused on overpriced digital art. But beneath the hype lies a deeper cultural signal: *people are reconfiguring ownership as identity performance.* Owning a Bored Ape, a CryptoPunk, or a dynamic identity token is no longer just about speculative gain—it is about signalling membership, worldview, and digital presence. These assets function as status badges, cultural shorthand, and in some cases, ideological markers. They represent a shift from money as a silent medium to money as an expressive one. And they are rewriting the rules of identity in real-time.

This leap is not without friction. Traditional states are wary of it, not merely for economic reasons but for ideological ones. Cryptographic ledgers introduce forms of permanence and portability that resist national boundaries. A Bitcoin wallet cannot be sanctioned in the same way as a bank account. A decentralised identity can persist across platforms, jurisdictions, and censorship regimes. These capabilities undermine the monopolies that institutions have long held over naming, recording, and verifying. When your assets, credentials, and reputation are stored on-chain, your economic self becomes unmoored from the state. And when enough people opt into that freedom, the very concept of citizenship begins to change.

Yet, while crypto destabilises traditional identity anchors, it also creates the conditions for new ones. Shared belief in a protocol becomes the glue that binds strangers. Online pseudonymity, long dismissed as a mask for bad behaviour, becomes a proving ground for trust earned through action rather than appearance. In this landscape, identity is no longer something assigned at birth; it is something performed, earned, and selectively revealed. This represents not just a technical innovation, but a philosophical one. It implies that *value and identity can be negotiated without permission.* And that is a cultural leap many institutions are structurally unprepared to absorb.

We must also reckon with the fact that cryptographic money, unlike coins or notes, is not a passive object—it is an active script. A coin holds value because we believe in the issuer. A smart contract holds value because we believe in its execution. This means that money is no longer merely carried—it is run. Like software. And with this shift comes new responsibilities. Errors in smart contracts can cost millions. Governance votes can reshape entire ecosystems. In this world, being economically literate is no longer enough. One must also be computationally and philosophically literate. Participation requires not just consumption, but interpretation.

This interpretive shift is perhaps the most important. When we moved from coins to codes, we moved from economies based on ritual to economies based on rules. But these rules, unlike state laws, are not written in legalese—they are written in logic. Immutable, transparent, and in many cases, unforgiving. If you lose your seed phrase, your assets vanish. If you approve a malicious contract, there is no recourse. In such a system, the user becomes the institution. And the institution is only as strong as the collective attention, comprehension, and care of its participants.

Which brings us to the final point: the leap from coins to codes is not just a leap in technology. It is a leap in accountability. It asks more of its users—more agency, more literacy, more awareness. But it also offers more in return. It offers the chance to co-author systems, to shape incentives, to exit legacy structures without waiting for reform. This is not something that traditional currency ever offered. You could spend a coin, but you could not edit it. You can fork a blockchain.

That is the cultural rupture. Crypto gives individuals not just the ability to opt out, but the tools to build something different. In doing so, it reframes money not as a fixed reality, but as an editable consensus. And when consensus can be rewritten by code, culture follows. Because wherever money flows, identity crystallises. And as we shift from coins to code, the very architecture of identity is being rewritten in real time—one protocol, one token, one block at a time.

Chapter 2
Proof of Belief – Building Conviction Before Capital

In markets that move at the speed of rumour, conviction has become a rare and fragile commodity. Most players don't pause to think—they simply react. The tempo of crypto trading, the barrage of competing narratives, and the endless stream of data points foster an atmosphere where knee-jerk moves get dressed up as strategy. Browse through any crypto forum or social feed and the pattern emerges quickly: opportunism presented as wisdom, volatility mistaken for vitality, and consensus reached before the facts have had time to settle. Yet beneath this clamour lies a slower, quieter skill—scarcer, and far more potent: the discipline to believe with intention. This chapter is about cultivating that discipline before you ever build a portfolio.

The crypto world is unusual not merely because it is decentralised or digital, but because it places exceptional weight on belief as a decision-making tool. Traditional finance leans heavily on institutional endorsements—ratings agencies, analysts, regulators, central banks. In crypto, such structures are either missing altogether or distrusted by design. There are no sanctioned gatekeepers to tell you what's legitimate. Few standards exist for separating quality from noise. The work of discernment falls squarely on the individual. And without the scaffolding of traditional authority, your most valuable asset is not a specific token, but a mind tuned to clarity.

Here, the idea of "proof of belief" becomes critical. Unlike "proof of work" or "proof of stake," this is not a blockchain protocol—it's a human process. It's the way you arrive at conviction not through hype or imitation, but through examination, patience, and hard reasoning. It's what enables you to tell the difference between a fleeting trend and a genuine signal. It's how you decide what to hold, what to ignore, and what to build upon—not because someone whispered it in a Telegram group, but because you've tested your assumptions and taken ownership of your conclusions.

The trouble is that conviction is often confused with confidence. They are not the same. Confidence is a performance—what you project outward, whether or not it's grounded. Conviction is inward—rooted in intellectual honesty, emotional steadiness, and the courage to slow your thinking when everyone else is in a sprint. In crypto, where a single hour's price action can induce both euphoria and despair, conviction is not merely helpful—it's a condition for survival.

Cultivating it, however, demands a deliberate pushback against the prevailing psychology of the space. Crypto is, by default, impatient. Its structure—real-time prices, round-the-clock trading, announcement frenzies, hype loops—rewards immediacy. To think long-term here is to swim against the current. It is to declare, "I will not outsource my decisions to trendlines or influencer threads. I will build a mental framework sturdy enough to withstand the noise." This mindset is not fostered by platforms that profit from your constant engagement, but it is precisely what separates genuine investing from mere speculation.

Long-term thinking in such an environment is radical. And it's not passive. It is an active form of patience—anchored not in inertia, but in purpose. Those who manage to stay the course over five or ten years in crypto don't get there by obsessively checking charts. They get there by understanding exactly what they've invested in, why it matters, and how it fits into a broader vision. They zoom out. They keep still when others are flailing. They endure the unease of uncertainty because they trust the reasoning that got them here. This is less about instinct and more about disciplined thought.

Yet discipline should not be mistaken for inflexibility. The road to conviction is lined with scepticism—but not cynicism. Scepticism is constructive; it asks questions, tests the edges, and holds off on belief until the evidence justifies it. It creates room for real insight. Cynicism, by contrast, is lazy. It dresses itself up as intelligence but shuns curiosity. Where the sceptic says, "Let's see what's beneath the surface," the cynic shrugs, "It's all rubbish," without lifting a finger to investigate. In crypto, cynicism can be especially seductive—often voiced by those who missed early wins and now rationalise their absence with contempt.

Intelligent doubt is an advantage. It stops you from being carried away by collective delusion. Market history is littered with examples of herd behaviour ending in collapse—from the South Sea Bubble to the dot-com bust to the altcoin mania of 2017. In each case, the fuel was not malice, but unexamined belief. People joined in because others were doing so. Prices climbed, not on improved fundamentals, but on self-feeding momentum. Without scepticism, belief becomes imitation—and in markets where narratives can be manufactured, that's dangerous ground.

Building conviction means engaging belief critically. It means testing your ideas under pressure, not shielding them behind slogans. It requires the ability to be wrong without unravelling, to change your stance without losing your bearings. Your portfolio should be more than a list of positions; it should map your thinking. Every holding should be anchored to a thesis. Every thesis should be able to survive a reasoned challenge. If you can't explain why you own something in a way that could persuade a thoughtful sceptic, you're not investing—you're hoping.

Which brings us to perhaps the most practical, and most demanding, task in this chapter: drafting your own thesis. In traditional finance, retail investors are rarely asked to articulate a personal investment philosophy. The assumption is that such thinking belongs to professionals. Crypto has dismantled that gate—but in the void it leaves, you need something sturdier than gut feeling. If you are to navigate with clarity, you must know not just what you believe, but why.

A thesis is not a price target. It's not even a trade plan. It is your interpretation of where and how value will emerge in this new financial order. Do you believe blockchains will replace current financial intermediaries? Then which ones, and over what time span? Do you think decentralised governance will outperform centralised control? Under what circumstances? Your thesis is your intellectual compass—it filters noise, directs your attention, and shields you from being emotionally hijacked by price swings.

More importantly, a thesis holds you accountable. It shifts you from reactive participation to deliberate engagement. It allows you to say,

"I made this choice not because it was fashionable, but because it aligns with my view of how value will evolve." And when the market turns—as it inevitably will—you'll be better able to interpret events, adapt your stance, or stand firm. That, in any discipline, is maturity: acting from comprehension, not compulsion.

None of this is a guarantee of success. Markets will surprise you. Black swans will appear. The aim is not perfection but resilience. Conviction doesn't mean certainty; it means you've thought deeply enough that uncertainty doesn't freeze you. It means holding multiple possibilities in mind without succumbing to panic or arrogance. It means operating in a decentralised economy without craving constant reassurance from centralised voices.

This chapter won't hand you a ready-made thesis. It will give you the tools to craft your own. It will explore how to think long in an attention-fuelled economy, how to sharpen scepticism without letting it rot into cynicism, and how to turn passive exposure into active comprehension. It's not about guessing which token will rocket next. It's about preparing your mind to work in a world where belief itself is a form of currency—and conviction, the only asset you truly own.

Because before you commit capital, you are already investing something more personal: your attention, your reputation, your decision-making process. Before you put your money at risk, you place your judgment on the line. And in this programmable economy—where value is not handed down but built in real time—that judgment is your greatest leverage. Use it wisely.

Beyond FOMO: Emotional Triggers in a Digital Gold Rush

The biggest risk in crypto isn't technical. It isn't smart contract exploits, rug pulls, or regulatory overreach. The most destabilising force in the digital asset space is far more intimate: *your own psychology*. The very traits that make humans adaptive—pattern recognition, social comparison, reward sensitivity—are the same traits that sabotage our decision-making in highly volatile, narrative-driven markets. In crypto, where information is fragmented, sentiment is tribal, and prices can double or collapse in hours, emotional discipline is not a soft skill—it is survival infrastructure.

To operate in this space without emotional awareness is to be caught in a behavioural whirlpool. You may believe you are acting rationally—applying logic, following research, trusting data—but more often than not, you are reacting. And those reactions are being driven by ancient circuits in the brain, calibrated not for digital markets but for tribal survival. Greed, envy, and urgency are not crypto phenomena. They are human defaults. Crypto just amplifies them with algorithmic precision.

Greed, in its rawest form, is the desire for more—more returns, more leverage, more velocity. In most asset classes, greed builds slowly. In crypto, it compounds rapidly. You see someone turn £1,000 into £100,000 with a meme coin you've never heard of. You read about a DeFi protocol yielding triple-digit APYs. You're told that this token—this one—is the future of finance. Each story plants a seed: maybe you're missing out. Maybe you're being too conservative. Maybe you're behind. Greed stops being about wealth creation and starts becoming a defence mechanism against imagined inadequacy.

Yet the most powerful driver behind this isn't purely greed. It's *envy*. Greed says, "I want that." Envy says, "I can't stand that *they* have it." In highly transparent digital ecosystems—where wallets, trades, and net worths can be publicly tracked—envy becomes ambient. It's not just that people are making money; it's that you can *see* exactly how they're doing it. Leaderboards, influencer threads, screenshot culture—all of these create a continuous loop of upward comparison. And comparison, unlike opportunity, is infinite. No matter how well you perform, someone else's outperformance becomes a referendum on your failure.

This effect is intensified by the time-compression of the crypto market. Because it runs 24/7, there is no market close to impose reflection or distance. There is no cooling-off period. Instead, you exist in a perpetual now—where the gap between action and reaction is razor-thin, and every minute not spent optimising feels like erosion. The result is a form of financial hypervigilance. Even sleep begins to feel like a liability. This is not investing. It is *emotional surveillance*—a constant checking of charts, feeds, and sentiment indicators, driven not by strategy but by fear of falling behind.

FOMO—fear of missing out—is often spoken about casually, but its mechanics are serious. At its root, FOMO is not just the fear of missing a trade. It is the fear of being *excluded from meaning*. In a culture where success is increasingly tied to early access—being whitelisted, being first in, being "early to the narrative"—missing out is not just a financial loss. It is a symbolic one. It implies you're not plugged in, not awake, not agile enough to win. This turns markets into identity validators. When that happens, every price movement becomes personal.

The challenge is not to eliminate emotion. That's neither possible nor desirable. Emotions contain information. They alert you to risk, opportunity, and values misalignment. But in markets like crypto, where the signal-to-noise ratio is low and narratives are weaponised for liquidity, the key is *emotional literacy*. It's being able to observe your emotional state without being overtaken by it. To ask: is this urgency coming from my thesis or from someone else's timeline? Is this fear a warning or a reflex? Am I reacting to data or to a story?

Understanding these questions requires more than mindfulness platitudes. It requires cognitive skill. For example, recognising the difference between *volatility* and *uncertainty* is crucial. Volatility is movement. Uncertainty is a lack of clarity about what that movement means. The problem is that humans interpret both as threats, triggering fight-or-flight responses that can lead to impulsive exits or reckless entries. But a volatile market that aligns with your thesis is not necessarily a bad sign—it may just be noise within your conviction zone. Without this framing, every dip becomes a crisis, and every pump a missed chance to maximise.

Similarly, understanding the *narrative cycles* of crypto is essential. Narratives in this space don't just explain reality—they *create* it. A protocol doesn't have to change anything fundamental to go up in price; it just needs to capture attention. But attention is finite, and as it rotates from sector to sector—NFTs to DeFi to L2s to memecoins—participants feel a pressure to rotate with it. This is often rationalised as diversification. But beneath the surface is a different urge: *alignment with the crowd.* The psychological need not to be left behind, not to be caught holding the wrong story when the music stops.

To build emotional awareness in this context is not to withdraw from the market. It is to participate with eyes wide open. It is to develop internal systems for interpreting urgency, filtering noise, and managing risk—not just financially, but cognitively. One practical method is to develop a *pre-commitment strategy*. Before entering any position, define your exit parameters—not just in terms of price, but in terms of thesis. Ask: what would make me change my mind about this asset? What event, if it occurred, would invalidate my belief? If you cannot answer that in advance, you will answer it in panic.

Another powerful filter is to track *emotional triggers* in real time. If you find yourself obsessively checking a token because others are talking about it, pause. Ask what you know beyond the price movement. Do you understand the protocol? Its roadmap? Its competitive context? If not, your action is not research—it is reactivity. Creating a habit of interrogating your own motivations reduces the risk of misreading the market through the lens of emotion.

There is also value in institutionalising reflection. Keeping a *crypto journal*—not for trades, but for *mindset*—can build a feedback loop between emotion and execution. Note what you were feeling before a decision. What you expected. What you feared. Then revisit those notes after the fact. You'll begin to notice patterns: tendencies to overestimate certain risks, to chase under pressure, to exit too soon from discomfort. The goal is not perfection. It is pattern recognition.

Ultimately, emotional awareness is not just defensive. It is strategic. In a market where overreaction is the norm, emotional composure becomes alpha. If you can sit through volatility without overtrading, you outperform. If you can resist FOMO while others scramble for entry, you gain entry on your terms. And if you can build conviction slowly—despite the pressure to act quickly—you end up owning not just assets, but understanding. That understanding compounds. It becomes a durable edge.

The digital gold rush of crypto creates emotional pressure that is easy to underestimate and hard to regulate. The tools available to traders—leverage, social signals, algorithmic dashboards—magnify the psychological stakes. But the underlying issue is not the tools. It is the unexamined psychology driving their use. Without conscious navigation, markets turn investors into reactors. With it, they become interpreters—not just of assets, but of themselves.

This chapter does not promise emotional mastery. But it argues that *emotional precision*—the ability to locate, name, and interrogate your own impulses—is as important as technical analysis or market research. It is a skill, not a trait. And like any skill, it improves with use. Crypto does not reward intelligence alone. It rewards *emotional agility paired with intellectual structure*. If you can build both, you are not just more likely to stay in the game—you are more likely to understand what game you're actually playing.

The Courage to Think Long

The most radical act in the crypto space isn't discovering a promising token before the crowd. It isn't deploying smart capital to arbitrage inefficiencies. It isn't even building a protocol that upends an incumbent industry. The most radical act is simply to wait—to see something clearly, understand it deeply, and hold conviction over time without folding to noise, volatility, or peer pressure. In a market optimised for short-termism, patience is rebellion.

This idea goes against the prevailing logic of the crypto ecosystem. The industry is structured to reward speed. Exchanges operate twenty-four hours a day, seven days a week, with global liquidity and frictionless access. Price movements are measured in seconds. Narrative cycles shift by the week. Token launches, airdrops, forks, and upgrades constantly fragment attention. Even the vocabulary betrays the tempo: degens, pumps, flips, snipes. What's prized is immediacy. What's punished is hesitation.

Within this environment, long-term thinking appears naive. Why hold when you can rotate? Why wait when you can chase the next narrative? But this surface logic conceals a deeper reality: *most people are not investing in crypto; they're participating in crowd psychology*. They're reacting to price signals, mirroring sentiment, and disguising speculation as strategy. Few have a thesis. Fewer still have the patience to let it mature. That's what makes patience so powerful. In a market where most participants are optimising for the next hour, thinking in terms of years creates a structural advantage.

Long-term thinking is not merely about time horizon—it's about mental posture. It's about choosing depth over velocity. Clarity over novelty. Substance over reaction. To think long is to decouple your beliefs from market noise. It is to understand the difference between volatility and invalidation. If a token drops 60% in a week, that tells you nothing about its long-term utility. It only tells you about short-term liquidity, positioning, and sentiment. Unless your thesis is tied to those forces, the price move is data—not instruction.

This is where the crypto space punishes clarity. The more you understand what you're holding, the more comfortable you become with temporary dislocation between price and value. But this requires epistemic courage: the willingness to act on knowledge that has not yet become consensus. The irony is that most people in crypto claim to be early. But very few are willing to *think* early—by which we mean before the trade is popular, before the story has been validated, before the chart has gone parabolic. Most want to be early with the benefit of hindsight. But long-term thinking demands that you tolerate discomfort now in exchange for conviction later.

This discomfort can take many forms. Psychological. Social. Financial. Watching a long-term thesis stagnate while others are chasing fast returns is an exercise in restraint. Seeing peers triple their portfolios on memecoins while you hold a governance token that no one is talking about tests your integrity. This isn't a matter of discipline alone—it's a matter of self-definition. Are you investing to impress, to win, or to build something that aligns with your beliefs?

Warren Buffett's oft-quoted wisdom—that the stock market is a device for transferring money from the impatient to the patient—is frequently cited in crypto but rarely practised. That's because the incentives are misaligned. Social media platforms reward constant visibility. Trading groups reward hyperactivity. Exchanges reward churn. If you're not posting positions, shilling bags, or sharing wins, it can feel like you're doing nothing. But that nothing—when it's grounded in clarity—is actually an edge. *Silence is a signal of internal structure.*

This is where the framing of time itself becomes critical. In crypto, time is often treated as a liability. Things move too fast. If you're not early, you're late. But from a long-term perspective, time becomes an asset. It becomes a filter that reveals what is real and what is not. A token that survives multiple market cycles, governance proposals, forks, and external shocks is fundamentally different from a token that rode a single narrative wave and vanished. Time filters hype. It kills weak projects. It rewards durability. But to benefit from that process, you must be willing to endure it.

Thinking long also changes how you evaluate opportunity. You begin to ask different questions. Not "What's pumping?" but "What's building?" Not "What's the narrative today?" but "What kind of problems will still matter five years from now?" You stop chasing answers and start cultivating frameworks. You learn to distinguish signal from attention. For example, developer activity, ecosystem resilience, treasury management, and governance participation become more important than short-term price action. These are the markers of foundational strength—not because they guarantee returns, but because they signal alignment with longevity.

This is also where long-term thinking intersects with ethics. When you think short, your decisions are extractive. You look to maximise return, often at the expense of context. But when you think long, your decisions become generative. You begin to care about the ecosystem's sustainability, the project's governance, the fairness of token distribution. You are no longer merely a trader. You are a stakeholder. This shift is not moralising—it's strategic. Healthy ecosystems produce more durable value than hype-driven ones. Your returns are not just a function of price, but of *what the price represents.*

Contrast this with the dominant culture of "exit liquidity." The idea that the purpose of crypto is to find someone dumber or later than you and offload your tokens before the collapse. This is not investing. It is opportunistic arbitrage masquerading as belief. It produces cycles of distrust, disillusionment, and short-termism. And it perpetuates the idea that crypto is just a casino, not a paradigm shift. But thinking long reframes your participation. You are no longer trying to win the game—you are trying to help design it.

This also changes how you deal with loss. A short-term mindset interprets every red candle as failure. A long-term mindset interprets drawdowns as data. What matters is whether your thesis has changed. Have the fundamentals evolved? Has the team shipped? Has the roadmap advanced? Has user adoption grown? If the answer is yes, then a 70% drop is not the end of belief—it is the test of it. This is not blind loyalty. It is informed resilience. The capacity to distinguish temporary setbacks from structural shifts.

There's also a meta-level to long-term thinking that deserves attention: how you define success in the first place. Is it a number in your portfolio? Is it early retirement? Is it the ability to teach others, to contribute meaningfully, to pass on financial literacy? Thinking long forces you to clarify these questions, because it connects capital to purpose. Without that connection, even your wins will feel hollow. You'll cash out, but remain restless. You'll have money, but not meaning. And meaning—especially in a decentralised world—is what gives capital its gravity.

In the end, thinking long in crypto is not about predicting the future. It's about designing your present around the kind of future you're willing to wait for. It is a commitment not to outcomes, but to process. To thinking slowly when others rush. To holding when others scatter. To asking better questions when others parrot narratives. It's an act of courage—not because it's heroic, but because it's rare. And in a market addicted to urgency, rarity is value.

Skepticism vs Cynicism

In markets shaped by speculation and storytelling, doubt is not a liability—it is a prerequisite for survival. Yet not all doubt is created equal. The ability to question, challenge, and withhold belief until evidence supports it is a skill that sharpens judgement. But when that same impulse calcifies into reflexive disbelief, it stops being productive and becomes corrosive. The difference between *skepticism* and *cynicism* is not just semantic—it's strategic. Understanding that difference is critical to building informed conviction in the crypto space, where hype and disillusionment often arrive hand in hand.

Skepticism is a posture of inquiry. It says: *Show me the logic. Help me understand the risk. Let me examine the assumptions before I commit my belief, my capital, or my credibility.* It invites inspection without assuming malice. It slows the mind down just enough to prevent narrative hijacking. Cynicism, by contrast, shuts that process down entirely. It pre-empts analysis by assuming the worst. The cynic sees fraud where the skeptic sees uncertainty. The cynic disengages to protect their ego; the skeptic engages to protect their integrity.

In crypto, the distinction has high stakes. Because the industry is young, decentralised, and minimally regulated, it attracts both visionaries and opportunists. There is no shortage of vapourware, dishonest actors, and empty promises. To navigate this landscape with your judgement intact requires doubt—but of the right kind. *Cynicism may shield you from scams, but it also blinds you to legitimate innovation.* It tells you that everything new is nonsense, that every ambition is a grift, that every risk is foolish. Over time, this perspective does not make you wiser—it just makes you static.

Take the example of Bitcoin in its early years. Many dismissed it outright—not because they had thoroughly assessed the whitepaper or understood the implications of decentralised consensus—but because the idea of non-governmental money seemed too absurd to be taken seriously. The cynics laughed. The skeptics asked, "What problem is this trying to solve?" The difference in approach led to a difference in opportunity. One group stayed on the sidelines. The other engaged with the idea, challenged it, studied it, and—eventually—some invested in it, not just financially, but intellectually. They built conviction before capital.

The same pattern repeated with Ethereum. Early critics scoffed at the idea of programmable money and self executing contracts. "It's just a platform for ICO scams," they said. And at times, they weren't wrong. But skepticism doesn't require blind faith—it requires selective openness. Ethereum skeptics acknowledged the noise but asked deeper questions: *What new behaviours do smart contracts make possible? What kinds of decentralised coordination might emerge if the technology matures?* These are the kinds of questions that expand understanding. The cynic dismisses the entire category. The skeptic refines it.

There is a psychological reason why cynicism often feels safer: it protects us from disappointment. If everything is a scam, nothing can surprise you. If no one is trustworthy, you're never betrayed. But this security is purchased at the cost of agency. The cynic opts out of analysis, out of learning, and ultimately, out of relevance. They confuse disengagement with insight. But real insight requires risk—not just the risk of being wrong, but the risk of having to change your mind.

Skepticism, by contrast, requires intellectual humility. It is grounded in the recognition that *you don't know yet.* It values process over posture. It acknowledges that even flawed ideas may contain seeds of progress, and that premature dismissal is often a function of limited understanding. Skepticism asks: what is the strongest version of this idea? What would I need to see in order to believe? These questions keep you open, without making you gullible.

This balance is especially important in crypto because so many ideas sound implausible at first. The concept of people coordinating across the world via pseudonymous identities and voting with tokens sounds outlandish—until you study DAOs. The notion of JPEGs selling for six-figure sums sounds irrational—until you understand how NFTs function as cultural capital in decentralised communities. These are not just technical innovations; they are new expressions of value, coordination, and belonging. To see them clearly, you must suspend disbelief *just long enough* to investigate.

That said, healthy skepticism is not passivity. It demands action: to read whitepapers, to analyse tokenomics, to inspect governance structures, to understand the technology stack. It requires you to dig—not just for flaws, but for *coherence.* Does the project's design match its stated ambition? Do incentives align across stakeholders? Is there transparency, responsiveness, and execution history? Skepticism uses doubt as a diagnostic tool. Cynicism uses it as a verdict.

This distinction also has interpersonal implications. Skeptics can engage with builders, critics, and fellow investors without losing their critical edge. Cynics struggle to engage at all. They scoff, dismiss, and isolate themselves from the very conversations that could expand their perspective. Ironically, this detachment often masquerades as superiority. But superiority without comprehension is not wisdom—it is intellectual insecurity in disguise. The strongest thinkers in the space are rarely the loudest sceptics or the first to call fraud. They are the ones asking careful questions, exploring multiple angles, and building mental models that evolve.

For those aiming to build conviction in the crypto space, this difference matters. Conviction born of cynicism is brittle. It's reactive, emotionally charged, and often short-lived. It exists to validate a narrative, not to test it. When challenged, it defends itself not with evidence but with sarcasm or retreat. Conviction born of skepticism, on the other hand, is resilient. It is the product of stress-tested belief. It is earned through exposure to disagreement, through reflection, and through iterative thinking. It welcomes challenge because it has been built to withstand it.

To develop this kind of conviction, you need a framework for applied skepticism. That means defining what constitutes credible evidence for you, what red flags you consider disqualifying, and what areas you're still actively learning. It means documenting your reasons for doubt—not to create a dossier of criticism, but to clarify your current boundaries of belief. Over time, these notes become invaluable. They show you how your thinking has evolved, where you were cautious, where you were wrong, and where you were justified. In volatile markets, this kind of intellectual journaling is a safeguard against reactive overcorrection.

This also means becoming comfortable with ambiguity. A skeptic doesn't need to reach a conclusion quickly. In fact, *good skepticism delays conclusion in favour of deeper understanding*. It treats uncertainty as an invitation, not a threat. In this way, skepticism becomes a way to build—not just defensively, but constructively. It helps you find the rare projects that deserve time, capital, and attention—not because they are flawless, but because they are coherent enough to warrant belief.

The reward for developing this kind of skepticism is not just better investment outcomes. It is a more nuanced relationship with belief itself. In decentralised systems, where the old markers of trust and legitimacy have been stripped away, your ability to think independently becomes your primary asset. But independence without insight is just arrogance. The goal is not to believe less, but to *believe more intelligently*. To do that, you must learn to doubt with precision. Not everything deserves your trust—but not everything deserves your contempt either.

This chapter is an invitation to refine your discernment. To treat skepticism not as a protective shell, but as a method of engagement. To ask better questions, to resist easy dismissal, and to train yourself to spot when doubt becomes a substitute for effort. Because the future of finance, like the future of belief, will be built not by the loudest sceptics, but by those who learn to think with clarity—even in uncertainty.

Writing Your Own Thesis

There is no shortage of information in crypto. Charts, dashboards, Twitter threads, newsletters, Discord channels, whitepapers—data flows constantly, often faster than anyone can reasonably absorb. But information is not conviction. And conviction, not information, is what shapes effective decision-making in volatile environments. Without it, the investor becomes a bystander—reactive, swayed by sentiment, beholden to trends they don't fully understand. Writing your own thesis is the process of transforming noise into narrative, speculation into strategy. It is the act of moving from passive consumption to active belief-building.

In the traditional financial world, retail participants are rarely encouraged to develop investment theses. Portfolio construction is outsourced to advisors, guided by models, or allocated by fund templates. Crypto offers no such scaffolding. There is no central authority to tell you what's reasonable, no index to hide behind, no universally accepted methodology for filtering risk. Instead, it demands agency. It puts the burden—and the opportunity—on the individual to decide what matters. A personal crypto thesis is not a luxury; it is your intellectual operating system. Without one, every price move is a test of your emotional resilience rather than your reasoning.

A thesis is not a list of price targets or a ranking of favourite tokens. It is not a bet on what's going to pump next. It is a framework: a coherent set of beliefs about where value will accrue in a decentralised economy, how innovation will unfold, and what principles guide your participation. It reflects your understanding of market structure, technology, governance, incentives, and human behaviour. It allows you to say not just *what* you're doing, but *why*—with a level of clarity that enables better timing, better sizing, and better resilience during volatility.

The first step in building this kind of thesis is to ask foundational questions—not about specific projects, but about systems. What do you believe is being disrupted? Is crypto primarily about replacing financial intermediaries? Creating censorship-resistant infrastructure? Unlocking new forms of coordination through tokens? Or is it about something more cultural—identity, participation, belonging? Each perspective points to different priorities. Someone who sees crypto as an evolution of capital markets will focus on DeFi primitives, protocol-level economics, and composability. Someone who views it as a cultural platform may gravitate toward NFTs, creator tools, and on-chain reputation. There is no single correct thesis—only coherent ones.

From here, the thesis should account for time. What are your expectations across short, medium, and long-term horizons? Are you building toward a three-year view or a thirty-year worldview? For example, you may believe that tokenised governance will become the norm for internet communities—but acknowledge that the tooling, legal frameworks, and UX are not yet mature. That belief may lead you to take early positions in DAO infrastructure protocols, even if adoption is currently shallow. The key is to differentiate between *thesis timing* and *market timing*. A thesis gives you permission to wait for the market to catch up—not in complacency, but in informed confidence.

Another critical dimension is your philosophy on risk. Crypto is an inherently uncertain space, full of false starts, speculative cycles, and technical complexity. What kinds of risk are you willing to take? Are you comfortable with volatility if it supports long-term vision? Do you prioritise decentralisation, even at the cost of speed? What are your non-negotiables—security guarantees, transparent tokenomics, credible teams? A well-formed thesis doesn't just point you toward opportunities. It helps you *filter out* what doesn't align, even when those things are trending. It's not only a compass—it's a boundary.

This filtering function is particularly important in crypto because attention moves faster than fundamentals. Narratives emerge, compound, and implode in days. Being early to a new sector—whether it's rollups, restaking, or zero-knowledge applications—can be lucrative. But without a thesis, you won't know *why* you're participating. You'll mistake narrative heat for structural significance. Your thesis gives you the ability to separate foundational innovation from speculative momentum. It lets you ask: Is this trend solving a real problem, or is it a new skin on an old idea?

To sharpen your thesis, it's essential to stress-test it. That means exposing it to contrary views, engaging with informed critics, and asking uncomfortable questions. What are the failure modes of your beliefs? What blind spots might you have? If the projects you believe in collapse, how would you interpret that failure? Would it invalidate your thesis, or simply require an update? These exercises are not academic. They build durability. Conviction that has not been interrogated is not conviction—it's inertia.

Articulating your thesis in writing is a necessary discipline. Thoughts that remain internal tend to be vague, circular, and overconfident.

Writing forces specificity. It reveals inconsistencies. It provides a reference point that can be revisited over time, refined in response to new data, or used to explain your views to others. If you can't explain your thesis clearly to a smart outsider, you likely don't understand it deeply enough. And if you can't explain it to yourself in a moment of market panic, you are more likely to abandon it under pressure.

This reflective process also serves as a defence against external noise. In crypto, there is always someone louder, earlier, richer. There is always a new chart, a new token, a new narrative. Without a thesis, every success you didn't capture feels like a personal failure. Every correction feels like proof you were wrong. But a thesis introduces internal coherence. It turns crypto from a game of reaction into a practice of interpretation. You are no longer looking for signals that match sentiment—you are looking for signals that match your thinking.

A strong thesis is never static. It evolves with your understanding. That's not a flaw—it's a feature. The goal is not to be dogmatic. It is to be deliberate. You should be able to update your thesis without abandoning its core. For example, you may start with a belief in the promise of decentralised exchanges, but adjust your thesis over time to reflect new insights about liquidity fragmentation or MEV exploitation. This is not flip-flopping. It is *strategic iteration*—learning in public, thinking in motion, while staying grounded in principle.

It's also important to recognise that writing a thesis is not limited to investors. Builders, contributors, creators, and researchers all benefit from a clearly articulated set of beliefs. Your thesis influences what you work on, who you collaborate with, how you allocate time and attention. In decentralised systems, where authority is distributed and legitimacy is fluid, personal clarity becomes more valuable than formal credential. Your thesis is your signal.

For some, this process may feel intimidating. But it is far less risky than the alternative—navigating a high-volatility market with borrowed conviction. Most investors don't fail because they choose the wrong token. They fail because they don't know why they chose it in the first place. Writing your thesis is not a guarantee of success. It is a hedge against confusion, against panic, against narrative dependence. It is the foundation upon which every meaningful decision can rest.

Start where you are. Write down what you believe about crypto today. What excites you? What worries you? What do you think others are missing? Then ask: what are you willing to risk for that belief? What would change your mind? What would make you double down? These are not abstract questions. They are tools of clarity. And clarity, in this space, compounds.

Because in a decentralised economy, no one is going to hand you conviction. You have to build it yourself. And building begins with articulation. With asking hard questions. With making your thinking visible—not for validation, but for refinement. Writing your thesis is the act of taking responsibility for your beliefs. It is what turns participation into purpose. And in a market driven by noise, that quiet clarity may be your most valuable asset.

Chapter 3
Digital Soil – Understanding What You're Really Investing In

Crypto investors are often trained to think in shorthand—tickers, price charts, market symbols. Yet these are only abstractions, and abstractions, by nature, conceal as much as they reveal. A coin is not a company. A protocol is not a product. A blockchain is not a vending machine that reliably dispenses value at the push of a button. Treating digital assets like a pile of interchangeable lottery tickets misses the deeper truth: you're not merely buying a thing, you're buying the economic soil it grows in. Soil that, if healthy, can sustain life, adapt under strain, and keep producing over the long haul. The real question isn't simply whether the ground is fertile, but whether you truly understand its composition.

This chapter urges a shift in perspective. The familiar surface metrics—market capitalisation, token price, 24-hour trading volume—are not causes; they are consequences. They describe behaviour, not the forces that drive it. To uncover the "why," you have to dig beneath the price action into the living system that lies underneath. And this is not just poetic licence. Ethereum, Solana, Avalanche, Cosmos—these are more akin to digital nations than mere coins. They have economies, governance structures, cultures, and even political tensions. Buying in is not simply exposure to volatility; it's a step inside a functioning, evolving ecosystem.

The distinction matters. In traditional finance, investors lean on quarterly reports, earnings, and balance sheets. In crypto, the equivalent data is far more fluid. "Revenue" might mean transaction fees or staking rewards. "Users" could be bots, DAOs, or pseudonymous wallets. Growth might emerge from cultural buzz as much as from technical innovation. No regulatory filing will tell you how Ethereum is faring. There's no single yardstick for the health of a decentralised network. Which is why crypto demands its own literacy—part economic, part technical, part anthropological.

To develop it, start with a deceptively simple question: what does this ecosystem make possible that wasn't possible before? Ethereum didn't succeed because it launched a token; it succeeded because it introduced a radically open model—permissionless programmability—that let developers create financial tools, governance frameworks, and ownership models directly on-chain. Solana, on the other hand, chased high throughput and low latency, enabling a different set of applications, communities, and compromises. Every layer-one protocol is, in effect, an invitation to inhabit a specific worldview. The architecture shapes the builders' incentives, the users' habits, and the governance dynamics. None of these choices are neutral, and neither are their consequences.

The savviest investors don't fixate on "the next big token." They ask: what economy is this protocol building? Who lives here? What are the rules? The strongest ecosystems are distinguished less by their token price than by the energy of their developer base, the maturity of their tools, the cohesion of their community, and their capacity to attract valuable applications. They grow like cities—messy, uneven, but patterned. Bitcoin is a fortified vault: slow, cautious, resistant to change. Ethereum feels more like a sprawling metropolis, always under construction. Solana resembles a high-speed transit hub—ideal for rapid experimentation, but less concerned with decentralised orthodoxy. None is inherently "better." What matters is knowing exactly what sort of wager you're making.

To find that clarity, you need to read the primary sources. In crypto, that's the whitepaper—a project's foundational text. Unlike glossy investor decks, whitepapers are often dense, technical, and aimed at builders rather than speculators. Reading them well requires patience and, more than technical mastery, discernment. What is the problem being solved? Is it pressing or theoretical? Does the architecture show a coherent vision, or is it a patchwork of fashionable terms? Some whitepapers drown in jargon; others are technically sound but strategically vague. Your task is to detect whether there's a real heartbeat beneath the complexity. If the whitepaper can't articulate why it should exist, no amount of clever tokenomics will make up for it.

Then there's the roadmap—not a list of promises, but a reflection of priorities. It reveals sequencing: which problems get addressed first, which upgrades are treated as urgent, how the team responds to new realities. A solid roadmap is not a straitjacket; it allows for iteration. You're not chasing certainty—you're seeking signal: the balance between vision and practicality, ambition and execution.

But documents only take you so far. The richer signals are found in the rituals that keep a network alive. Developer calls. Governance votes. Hackathons. AMAs. GitHub commits. These are not just PR stunts—they are the culture in motion. They show whether momentum is organic or propped up by hype. Rituals embed shared identity, and in crypto, identity is capital. If no one turns up to vote, the DAO is hollow. If proposals stop flowing, the treasury becomes inert. In a decentralised network, participation is not a side metric—it's the mechanism through which the future is decided.

Some of the most telling indicators don't appear on CoinMarketCap at all. How many developers are actively contributing code—not just downloading it? How fast is the tooling improving? Does the team engage with its community or operate in isolation? Are grants flowing to builders, or gathering dust in a multisig wallet? Such questions reveal what the protocol truly values, as opposed to what it merely claims to.

And then there's the social layer—the memes, inside jokes, and shared symbols. It may look frivolous from the outside, but it's anything but. Memes act as cultural glue and narrative accelerants. They shape perception, foster belonging, and reinforce coordination. A strong meme culture can indicate a community's ability to rally around shared goals. This doesn't mean every project needs a mascot; it means that stories and symbols are infrastructure. Ethereum's "ultrasound money" wasn't just a gag—it reframed its monetary policy. Bitcoin's "HODL" wasn't merely a typo—it became a creed. Dismiss this at your peril; you risk overlooking how belief—and thus trust—is formed.

By weaving together the technical architecture, the clarity of documentation, the pulse of governance, the activity of contributors, and the vibrancy of culture, you begin to see an ecosystem as a whole organism. Not a speculative product, not a number on a chart, but a living economy. This is no abstract exercise—it directly informs how you deploy capital, judge risk, and spot long-term potential. It shows you when a project's lively market is masking deeper decay, or when a small, underestimated network is quietly preparing for explosive growth. Once you understand the soil, you stop chasing flowers—you start planting trees.

That's the work ahead: learning to read beyond the coin, to trace intention through documents, to treat participation as a leading indicator. It means replacing the question "What should I buy?" with "What could this ecosystem become, and what role could I play in it?" In crypto, price is just noise. Structure is the true signal. And if you want conviction that lasts, you have to dig—not for treasure, but for roots.

Layers of Value: Blockchain Beyond Bitcoin

For most new entrants to the crypto space, value appears deceptively simple: it is what a token is worth on the open market. Bitcoin is valuable because people are willing to pay thousands of dollars per unit. Ethereum's value can be tracked on a chart, updated in real time. These numbers fluctuate, sometimes wildly, and the story seems to be written in price. But this narrative—while convenient—is intellectually shallow and strategically dangerous. Market capitalisation is not value; it is a reflection of temporary consensus. To understand the real value of blockchain networks, one must look beyond coins and begin to understand *layers*—the hidden architecture that sustains, extends, and multiplies worth across time, communities, and use cases.

Bitcoin was the first digital asset to prove that distributed trust could be monetised. Its genius was in turning raw belief—anchored in cryptographic security and enforced by distributed consensus—into a tradeable unit. But Bitcoin is structurally narrow by design. Its goal is singular: to be decentralised money. Ethereum, and the ecosystems that followed, asked a broader question: what else can blockchains do? The answer gave rise to a layered model of value creation. Unlike traditional assets that are often evaluated through financial ratios or profit forecasts, blockchain-based systems derive their worth from a confluence of technological robustness, economic utility, and social participation. *Value in crypto is emergent, layered, and contextual—rarely visible at first glance.*

At the most foundational level sits *infrastructure*. This is where value begins—not with the apps you interact with, but with the protocols that make those interactions possible. These are the base layers: Bitcoin, Ethereum, Solana, Avalanche, and others. They provide the security guarantees, consensus mechanisms, and decentralised computation needed to operate trustless systems. The stability, throughput, and design choices of these base layers determine the ceiling for what can be built on top. For instance, Ethereum's choice to prioritise decentralisation and composability over raw speed has shaped its ecosystem into a hub for DeFi, NFTs, and DAOs. In contrast, Solana's high-throughput design enables rapid-fire transactions but comes with different trade-offs around node participation and reliability. Understanding these foundational attributes is essential. *An application inherits the strengths and weaknesses of the chain it lives on.*

However, infrastructure alone is not enough. The next layer is *utility*—where raw capability is translated into functional products. These are the smart contracts, applications, protocols, and bridges that users actually engage with. In DeFi, this includes lending platforms like Aave, decentralised exchanges like Uniswap, and yield optimisers like Yearn. In NFTs, utility manifests through marketplaces, minting tools, and creator royalties. In gaming, it's the token economics, item ownership mechanics, and interoperability frameworks that matter. But utility must be evaluated not just on what is *promised*, but what is *used*. A protocol may claim to enable global payments, but if its actual daily volume is negligible, the utility is theoretical. Conversely, even simple tools that solve real user problems—such as MetaMask for wallet interaction—can accumulate immense value by becoming infrastructure in their own right. *The key is adoption, not ambition.*

Yet the story is still incomplete without the third layer: *community*. This is perhaps the most misunderstood component of value in crypto, particularly by traditional investors. A community is not just a Telegram group or a Discord server. It is the network of developers who build, users who evangelise, holders who fund, and thinkers who evolve the culture of a protocol. Community provides continuity. In decentralised systems, there is no CEO to steer the ship—only contributors who choose to show up, vote, write proposals, merge code, and organise meetups. Projects with mediocre tech but strong community often outperform, because communities *create resilience.* They help absorb shocks, respond to crises, and iterate on direction. Ethereum survived The DAO hack, contentious forks, and regulatory scrutiny not because of a genius founder, but because of a distributed community with conviction. Without community, infrastructure and utility eventually degrade into abandoned code.

To assess the community layer, you must look beyond Twitter metrics or wallet addresses. Examine governance participation. Review contributor activity on public repos. Look at retention—not just how many joined during the bull run, but how many stayed through the drawdown. Is the conversation in the community technical, ideological, mercenary, or chaotic? Are participants aligned around a mission, or just a meme? Do they correct misinformation, or amplify it? These behavioural indicators provide a clearer sense of long-term value than most tokenomics spreadsheets.

Crucially, these layers are not independent. They are *interdependent systems.* Infrastructure without utility becomes technical theatre. Utility without community becomes a ghost town. Community without infrastructure collapses under its own weight. Value in crypto is strongest when all three layers reinforce each other.

Consider the case of Ethereum: its infrastructure has been battle-tested, its utility continues to expand across use cases, and its community is among the most ideologically coherent and technically sophisticated. This doesn't mean it is invincible. But it does mean its value is not speculative fantasy—it is structurally grounded.

Contrast this with short-lived tokens that balloon during hype cycles. These may show temporary price action, but when you peel back the layers, they are often hollow. Infrastructure is copied, utility is untested, and community is opportunistic. These projects can rise fast, but they fall just as quickly—because they lack the layered resilience that defines sustainable ecosystems. *Real value is not what pumps—it is what persists.*

The layered model also offers a practical framework for evaluating emerging projects. When you discover a new token, ask: what layer does this project operate on? Does it enhance infrastructure, provide new utility, or strengthen a community? What dependencies does it have? For example, a new Layer-2 scaling solution might rely on Ethereum's security but introduce its own execution model and fee structure. A DAO tooling project might not be flashy, but if it enables more efficient governance, it can quietly become foundational. Understanding these dynamics helps you allocate not just capital, but *attention*—a scarcer and more influential resource in digital economies.

There are also temporal dynamics to consider. Value shifts across layers depending on the market cycle. During speculative booms, attention often flocks to utility—new protocols, yield farms, token launches. But in downturns, infrastructure tends to matter more. This is when teams refine architecture, clean up debt, and prepare for the next wave. Community also becomes visible in bear markets: who is still building, contributing, and participating when incentives dry up? These transitions are not just cycles—they are stress tests for each layer's integrity.

Importantly, these layers are not confined to protocols. The same framework applies to people. As a participant in crypto, whether investor, builder, or researcher, you also operate across layers. Your infrastructure is your knowledge base—how well you understand the core technologies. Your utility is what you contribute—capital, code, content, governance. Your community is who you collaborate with—your peers, mentors, DAOs, and social graphs. The stronger these layers are in your own engagement, the more effective—and resilient—you will be over time.

Value in crypto, then, is not a singular object to be discovered. It is a *composite structure* to be understood. This requires intellectual depth, critical attention, and patience. It demands that you look past surface narratives and interrogate what lies beneath. It asks you to think in systems, not in symbols. In a market that often rewards simplicity and speed, this layered thinking is a competitive advantage. Because while the price may show you what the crowd believes today, the layers tell you what will matter tomorrow.

Ecosystems, Not Coins

When most people first enter the world of crypto, they come looking for a coin. They ask about the price of Ethereum, the potential of Solana, or whether Cardano is "undervalued." The assumption is clear: these are discrete products competing for market share—like stocks in a technology index, or brands in a consumer market. But this framing misses the essence of what these networks represent. Ethereum is not a product. Solana is not a single business. These are not coins in the traditional financial sense; they are *economies*. They are digital nations, complete with infrastructure, citizens, governance models, financial systems, legal code, and cultural identity. To evaluate them properly is to understand them as *living ecosystems*—fluid, participatory, and continuously co-constructed by their communities.

Treating a blockchain protocol like a company encourages a shallow analysis. Traditional frameworks such as price-to-earnings ratios, user acquisition costs, or gross margins simply don't apply. There is no central revenue model. There is no CEO issuing quarterly earnings. What exists instead is an open-source, decentralised platform upon which value is created not by the protocol itself, but by the people building, transacting, governing, and contributing to it. Ethereum, for example, did not grow in value because Vitalik Buterin executed a brilliant product strategy. It grew because thousands of developers built DeFi protocols, NFT marketplaces, governance DAOs, and privacy tools on top of it—making it indispensable infrastructure. *Value in crypto networks accrues not through top-down planning but through bottom-up emergence.*

This is the fundamental shift: blockchains are not digital corporations; they are digital states. Just as a nation's GDP is not the product of its government but of its economic participants, a blockchain's vitality stems from its capacity to support meaningful activity. When you assess a blockchain, you are not just evaluating its codebase or throughput. You are asking: who lives here? What do they build? How do they govern themselves? What values do they hold? What tools do they use? *Every blockchain is a political, economic, and social experiment*—not just a technical one.

Consider Ethereum. It functions more like a constitutional monarchy than a corporation. There are influential figures—core developers, thought leaders, and early contributors—but no central authority. It has its own system of taxation (gas fees), its own legal mechanisms (smart contracts), its own monetary policy (ETH issuance and burning), and its own currency (ETH). Developers, users, and DAOs form the economic base. Validators enforce rules, akin to a decentralised judiciary. Governance is partially on-chain, partially informal, echoing the dynamics of constitutional conventions more than executive boards. Understanding Ethereum's trajectory means studying not just code updates, but cultural evolution—how its community resolves conflicts, debates values, and integrates change.

Now look at Solana. Unlike Ethereum's slow, deliberative consensus culture, Solana's ethos is one of speed, experimentation, and throughput. Its architecture prioritises high-frequency, low-cost transactions, attracting developers focused on consumer applications, gaming, and high-volume DeFi. Its community prizes performance and scale. The values are different, the incentives are different, the risks are different. To treat Solana and Ethereum as interchangeable "Layer 1s" is like comparing Singapore to Switzerland based solely on GDP figures. *Their core philosophies, governance structures, and development paths differ radically*—and those differences shape long-term viability.

This ecosystem lens also exposes why token price is often a misleading indicator. In a nation, the value of a currency may rise or fall due to speculative flows, but it doesn't necessarily reflect the strength of the economy. A thriving export sector, stable legal institutions, and a well-educated workforce matter more. Similarly, a token may pump due to hype or external market conditions, but unless the underlying ecosystem is producing tools, value, and governance capacity, the price is unsustainable. *Speculation is not the enemy—but it must be distinguished from structural health.*

To assess a blockchain as an economy, one must evaluate four key dimensions. First, *developer activity*: how many people are building, and what are they building? GitHub commits, hackathon participation, ecosystem grants, and composability across protocols are critical indicators. Second, *user engagement*: how many active addresses are interacting with protocols daily? Are these users retained, or are they mercenaries following airdrops and yield? Third, *governance participation*: do token holders meaningfully engage in shaping protocol rules? Is there transparency in proposals and voting mechanisms? Fourth, *network resilience*: how has the ecosystem responded to outages, hacks, forks, or regulatory threats? Each of these factors reveals more about a blockchain's durability than any market cap ranking.

Importantly, ecosystems develop cultural identities. Ethereum has a strong bias toward credible neutrality and decentralisation. It is governed by a slow, almost academic culture that values robustness over novelty. Solana celebrates iteration and application-layer experimentation. Avalanche prioritises subnets and customisability. Cosmos advances interoperability and sovereignty. These identities are not marketing slogans; they are behavioural patterns that influence which developers stay, which users trust the system, and how innovation is channelled. Just as nations form identities over time, so too do digital economies—and these identities affect everything from incentive design to community retention.

Understanding blockchains as economies also clarifies why "Ethereum killers" have mostly failed to kill Ethereum. Competing on features—lower fees, faster transactions, better UI—is not enough. One must also replicate the developer mindshare, ideological cohesion, and governance maturity that Ethereum has accrued over years of iterative trust-building. This is not a technical challenge; it is a *social one.* You can fork Ethereum's codebase in an afternoon. You cannot fork its community, its norms, or its reputation. These are earned through participation, not innovation alone.

This paradigm also helps us interpret new chains more thoughtfully. When a new Layer 1 emerges, the immediate question should not be "what's the TPS?" or "how's the tokenomics?" The real questions are: who is migrating here? What problems does this community want to solve? What social contracts are forming? What primitives are being built that others might rely on? Adoption is not an engineering problem—it's a cultural one. *Technological potential without ecosystem traction is just architecture in search of meaning.*

Digital nations also export and import value. Just as countries trade goods, services, and culture, blockchains integrate through bridges, standards, and shared protocols. Ethereum-based tokens can be bridged to Arbitrum or Avalanche. DAOs can coordinate across chains using governance interfaces like Snapshot. NFTs created on one chain can be displayed and transacted on others. This interoperability does not erase identity—it magnifies it. Just as globalisation has made national identity more pronounced, interoperability forces blockchain communities to clarify their values, strengths, and unique contributions. Ecosystems are not isolated—they are *nodes in an emerging meta-economy.*

All of this points to a crucial mindset shift: investing in a token is not buying a piece of a company. It is *joining a digital economy.* You are choosing to participate in a network, share its values, adopt its currency, and contribute to its governance. The token is not just a financial instrument; it is a passport, a vote, and a claim on collective effort. This requires a more holistic diligence process—one that balances technical due diligence with cultural intelligence and economic intuition. Investors who fail to grasp this will continue to chase short-term gains while missing the deeper tectonic shifts underway.

Ultimately, the most valuable blockchains will not be the ones with the most impressive whitepapers or the flashiest marketing. They will be the ones that prove themselves as *functional digital economies*: with productive contributors, transparent institutions, resilient governance, and adaptive social contracts. Projects like Ethereum and Solana are not just networks—they are experiments in digital civilisation. To invest in them wisely is to understand not just where the code is heading, but where the culture is going.

Whitepapers, Roadmaps, and Rituals

One of the most enduring myths in crypto investing is the assumption that reading a whitepaper is an adequate substitute for real diligence. Like business plans in the early dot-com days, whitepapers have become a ceremonial document—equal parts technical explainer, philosophical manifesto, and marketing tool. But unlike peer-reviewed academic papers or regulated financial prospectuses, whitepapers are unstandardised, unaudited, and often strategically vague. The question, then, is not whether a project has a whitepaper, but whether the document reveals anything meaningful about its intent, architecture, or ethos. *In a space fuelled by narrative, discerning signal from style is an essential skill.*

At its best, a whitepaper can offer insight into the intellectual scaffolding of a project. Bitcoin's original paper—just nine pages, written in unadorned prose—was revolutionary not just because of the code it inspired, but because of the clarity and restraint it demonstrated. It didn't oversell. It didn't promise the moon. It presented a coherent argument for a decentralised timestamp server that solved a long-standing problem in distributed computing. Its elegance was its credibility. Contrast this with many modern crypto whitepapers, which often drown in buzzwords and speculative features—layering zero-knowledge proofs atop cross-chain liquidity incentives with gamified staking mechanisms, all in the name of "next-gen Web3."

The issue is not complexity per se, but opacity. A technically sophisticated whitepaper can be valuable, but only if it communicates clearly. What problem is this project trying to solve? Why does blockchain make that solution better? What are the trade-offs? What assumptions are being made about users, incentives, scalability, and governance? If these questions are not addressed with precision and humility, the whitepaper becomes less a design document and more a smokescreen. *Complexity without clarity is often a red flag—not a badge of innovation.*

Then there is the roadmap. A roadmap is meant to express a project's intentions: what it plans to build, when, and how. In practice, many roadmaps are aspirational timelines backed by little operational insight. They function more like promises than plans—designed to instil confidence, attract funding, and buy time. The irony is that the more detailed the roadmap, the more likely it is to become obsolete. Markets shift. Tech stacks evolve. Regulatory threats emerge. And yet, the absence of a roadmap can suggest lack of structure or commitment. This creates a dilemma: how do we read a roadmap critically, without either overvaluing it or dismissing it entirely?

The answer lies in how a project handles deviation. *Adaptability is more important than accuracy.* A healthy project treats its roadmap not as gospel, but as an evolving contract with its community. It communicates changes, explains delays, and iterates publicly. Watch how a team responds when milestones slip. Do they hide? Blame externalities? Or do they engage transparently, offering revised timelines and justifications? The roadmap is not the point; the reflexive honesty around it is. Projects that can't ship on time are common. Projects that pretend nothing has changed are dangerous.

Beyond the documents themselves, we enter the world of *rituals*—the regular, often informal practices that shape a project's cultural and operational rhythm. In traditional organisations, this might include quarterly earnings calls, team stand-ups, or annual retreats. In crypto, rituals take many forms: governance forums, protocol upgrade votes, AMAs, hackathons, Discord debates, and meme propagation. These rituals reveal how a community communicates, resolves conflict, rewards contribution, and negotiates direction. They are the heartbeat of the project's social layer—and they matter as much as the code.

Take Ethereum's core developer calls: public, recorded, and often meandering. They reveal not just technical progress but the social dynamics of the network's stewards. Disagreements are aired, not buried. Consensus is earned, not enforced. Compare this with centralised Layer 1s where protocol changes happen behind closed doors and are announced fully formed. The difference is not just procedural; it's philosophical. One prioritises legitimacy through deliberation, the other through velocity. The rituals reflect the governance values—transparency, inclusion, authority—which in turn shape the long-term sustainability of the ecosystem.

Whitepapers and roadmaps might declare a project's values. Rituals show whether those values are lived. Consider how token distribution is conducted. Is there a fair launch or a pre-sale with preferential allocations? Are governance rights equitably distributed, or are they concentrated in a foundation or VC consortium? These aren't just economic details—they are design decisions with moral implications. *Crypto is not value-neutral.* Every line of code encodes assumptions about who has power, who gets rewarded, and how dissent is handled. Documentation that fails to address these dimensions is incomplete.

Even marketing artefacts—launch videos, websites, influencer partnerships—carry informational weight. A project that invests more in brand than in GitHub commits may be signalling its priorities. Is the team doxxed? Are contributors active in public discourse? Are audits conducted and published? These are not bureaucratic boxes to tick; they are manifestations of culture. A well-crafted whitepaper with no live code is a manifesto, not a protocol. A detailed roadmap without updates is theatre. Rituals without substance are fanfare.

Critical analysis means looking beyond the page. Who wrote the whitepaper? Was it the actual builders, or a third-party copywriting agency? Does the roadmap reference real developer milestones, or is it built around token releases and price catalysts? Do the rituals include community input, or are they one-way broadcasts from the founding team? Ask not just what the documents say, but what they imply—and more importantly, what they omit.

In evaluating documentation, we must also guard against confirmation bias. Many investors read whitepapers not to understand, but to justify. They seek language that validates their prior beliefs. The more complex the prose, the easier it is to project value onto it. The antidote is intellectual humility: *reading to learn, not to affirm*. Good documentation invites scrutiny. It explains trade-offs. It resists overpromising. If you walk away from a whitepaper more confused than when you started, that's not a sign of sophistication. It's a warning.

Documentation should also be read longitudinally. The original whitepaper is a starting point, not a final word. How has the protocol evolved since its launch? Has the team stuck to its stated vision, or pivoted repeatedly in response to market trends? Revisions, blog posts, governance proposals, and community calls are all part of the extended documentation. Read them like a historical record. Track the gap between stated ambition and realised action. *The delta between vision and execution is where trust lives or dies.*

Finally, understand that documentation is performative. It is meant to persuade, to inspire, and often to raise capital. That does not make it disingenuous—but it demands interpretation. Learn to read like an anthropologist: decoding not just what is said, but why it is said that way, and what it tells you about the social fabric of the protocol. Good projects want to be understood. Great projects structure their communication so that outsiders *can* understand. The rest rely on opacity, distraction, and momentum.

In the end, whitepapers, roadmaps, and rituals are not accessories to a protocol—they are windows into its soul. They are how decentralised systems declare identity, invite trust, and coordinate belief. In a world with no central authority, documentation becomes a new kind of contract—part vision, part commitment, part mirror. Reading it well requires more than technical literacy. It requires cultural fluency, emotional intelligence, and a willingness to interrogate not just what you are buying into, but who you are becoming by doing so.

The Invisible Metrics of Worth

The visible price of a token is often the least interesting thing about it. Market capitalisation, daily volume, and price charts offer immediate signals—but they are also lagging indicators, shallow reflections of deeper activity. In the short term, they can be gamed, manipulated, or inflated through speculative cycles. In the long term, they often conceal more than they reveal. The deeper value of a blockchain ecosystem—its resilience, adaptability, and cultural relevance—lives in subtler, more telling places. *To understand where real crypto value emerges, one must learn to read what isn't on the homepage of a price aggregator.*

A good place to start is with developer activity. Not all code commits are created equal, but sustained open-source development is still one of the clearest signs that an ecosystem is alive and evolving. GitHub repositories, for example, offer a transparent record of a project's technical momentum. Are developers actively pushing updates? Are bugs being triaged and fixed? Is the roadmap being translated into code? While vanity commits and automated scripts can inflate these figures, meaningful indicators—like the number of independent contributors, velocity of meaningful pull requests, and breadth of ecosystem tooling—cannot be faked over time. *A blockchain without builders is a monument, not a movement.*

Developer activity also tells us about a project's gravitational pull. Strong developer communities form around fertile environments—ones that offer documentation, grants, modular architecture, and shared ethos. Ethereum, for example, continues to attract thousands of independent developers not because it's the fastest or cheapest chain, but because it is legible, open-ended, and ideologically coherent. Its tooling stack, community support, and sense of purpose create a self-sustaining flywheel of experimentation. Contrast this with projects that announce million-dollar developer funds, but struggle to inspire real engagement. *Money might buy temporary interest, but purpose sustains attention.*

Next comes governance structure, a dimension too often neglected by retail investors. How decisions are made in a decentralised ecosystem—who proposes changes, who votes on them, and how outcomes are enforced—shapes everything from protocol upgrades to community morale. On-chain governance may seem like an abstract concern, but it directly impacts investor protection, innovation velocity, and ecosystem legitimacy. Poorly designed governance often leads to cartelisation, apathy, or capture by a vocal minority. In contrast, well-structured governance creates a robust dialogue between developers, users, and token holders—ensuring that the protocol evolves in alignment with its values.

Consider the differences between unilateral control and collective stewardship. A chain governed entirely by a founding team may iterate faster, but it also risks becoming brittle, authoritarian, or legally vulnerable. One that delegates all power to token-weighted votes can drift into plutocracy or voter fatigue. The nuance lies in hybrid models—quadratic voting, council-based systems, off-chain signalling, or rotating multisig teams—that aim to balance efficiency with legitimacy. *Governance is not just a feature—it is a mirror of collective intent.* It tells us whether a project aspires to be a product, a public good, or a political experiment.

Then there is meme culture—perhaps the most misunderstood, yet most potent invisible metric in crypto. Dismissed by outsiders as frivolous, memes are in fact cultural algorithms. They compress complex narratives into emotionally resonant, easily transmissible formats. Memes are how communities signal belonging, reinforce conviction, and transmit values. A protocol with a vibrant meme culture isn't just having fun—it's demonstrating coherence, energy, and internal morale. *Memes are social consensus in motion.* They are not jokes; they are operating systems of belief.

Take Dogecoin. Its meme-first identity was not an accident—it was a form of commentary on the absurdity of financial systems, packaged in irony and community joy. That cultural capital translated into sustained engagement, celebrity endorsements, and eventually, liquidity. Or look at Solana's "breakpoint" memes, which manage to capture both self-awareness and ambition. When memes emerge organically—when they're not crafted by marketing teams, but by participants—they become artefacts of emergent order. *You cannot manufacture meme culture; you must earn it.*

Another invisible but vital metric is composability. This refers to how easily different applications within an ecosystem can plug into one another, building upon shared infrastructure. Ethereum's strength lies in the interoperability of its protocols—lending platforms talking to decentralised exchanges, wallets integrating with NFTs, DAOs managing treasuries via smart contracts. Composability accelerates innovation because it allows teams to focus on specific components, trusting others to build adjacent modules. It creates network effects not through branding, but through architectural integrity. If developer activity shows that people are building, composability shows *how* well they're building together.

Let us also consider contributor diversity. Projects heavily reliant on a single team or company, no matter how talented, are inherently fragile. When leadership churns or funding dries up, progress stalls. But ecosystems with distributed talent, community-led initiatives, and multiple core teams exhibit anti-fragility. They can withstand shocks, navigate disagreement, and evolve organically. Look not just at who's coding, but who's educating, designing, funding, auditing, and governing. *The decentralisation of labour is as critical as the decentralisation of control.*

Social resilience is another underappreciated dimension. How does a community respond to failure, criticism, or security incidents? Does it fracture, lash out, or introspect? Does it learn in public, adapt, and improve? Every ecosystem faces moments of reckoning—whether through exploit, bear market, or internal conflict. These moments test more than technology; they test *culture.* A mature community absorbs setbacks without losing its centre. An immature one dissolves into blame or silence. *Resilience isn't visible in good times. It's revealed in crisis.*

Finally, we must talk about transparency—specifically, how consistently a project communicates not just wins, but trade-offs, limitations, and mistakes. Is the treasury public? Are team wallets labelled? Are smart contract audits published and kept up to date? Is there a record of governance participation and voting outcomes? Transparency builds trust not because it guarantees virtue, but because it allows informed judgement. *Opacity is a choice. So is clarity.*

None of these metrics—developer activity, governance architecture, meme vitality, composability, contributor diversity, social resilience, transparency—show up on a candlestick chart. They don't appear on CoinMarketCap or feature prominently in token price analyses. But over time, they are the scaffolding upon which durable value is built. They are the slow, invisible work that transforms hype into substance. *If capital is the fuel, these are the engines.*

To evaluate them, you need a different kind of literacy. Not just financial or technical, but cultural. You must learn to read GitHub like a newsroom, Twitter like a constitution, memes like manifestos. You must ask not only "What is this project worth today?" but "What kind of world is this project trying to build, and how earnestly is it doing so?" This requires time, attention, and the courage to form your own thesis—not one borrowed from influencers, Discord groups, or price charts.

The most important truths in crypto are not shouted; they're whispered in metrics that don't always have dashboards. They live in documentation footnotes, community forums, dev calls, and in the tone of public dialogue. They reveal whether a project is building for the next cycle, or for the next generation. Price is what you pay; value is what you understand. And the deeper your lens into the invisible, the more clearly you'll see what others overlook.

Chapter 4
The Architecture of Belonging – Communities, Cults, and Networks:

There is a peculiar irony in our so-called decentralised future: the more technology dismantles the old scaffolding of trust, the more it drives us to seek out new forms—often more tribal, symbolic, and emotionally charged than the institutions we've left behind. Cryptocurrency, born as a protocol for peer-to-peer exchange, has grown into something far more anthropological. It is no longer simply about decentralised ledgers and programmable assets. It is about belonging—about weaving identity, meaning, and solidarity in digital space. Beneath every token chart, behind the cycles and market metrics, lies a disarmingly simple question: with whom do we choose to build, and to believe?

Here, the focus shifts from what crypto does—economically, technically, politically—to what it means. And meaning, as historians of religion or sociology would remind us, is inseparable from community. The architecture of belonging—how people gather, align, mythologise, and commit—is not a decorative layer in crypto. It is its engine. Projects don't just succeed on code, capital, or regulatory clearance; they live or die by their ability to cultivate communities willing to believe with enough fervour to build, govern, and persist.

At the centre of this cultural engine are memes—not as fleeting internet jokes, but as structural components of monetary systems. In crypto, memes are not marketing garnish. They are belief protocols. They are light, fast, and emotionally adhesive, serving as a consensus layer for decentralised tribes. Through symbols, catchphrases, and rituals, memes compress ideology into forms that spread without the cumbersome weight of formal doctrine. The lightning bolt of Doge. The laser eyes. The ubiquitous "wagmi." None of these are incidental. Each is an accelerant of cohesion. If blockchains are the rails, memes are the combustible fuel.

It's hardly a new phenomenon. Religious movements, political uprisings, and early nation-states have long leaned on iconography and narrative shorthand to galvanise belief. Yet in crypto's native digital ecosystem, the effect is magnified. Here, memes are not only cultural markers—they are market movers. They can dictate valuations, influence liquidity, and, at times, sustain a project with narrative force alone. A project rich in memetic resonance can attract developers, investors, and ideological allies at a speed that more technically capable—but narratively bland—alternatives cannot match. Culture, once a soft variable, is now a price-sensitive input.

This raises a deeper question: how do we organise trust when the traditional arbiters of legitimacy no longer command default respect? One emerging answer comes in the form of DAOs—Decentralised Autonomous Organisations—which are less about novel governance mechanics and more about novel social architecture. DAOs reject the rigid hierarchies of companies and their shareholder primacy in favour of token-weighted participation, community voting, and rule sets embedded in code. In theory, they allow for coordination without centralised control. In reality, they mirror the frictions, aspirations, and ideological experiments of a generation designing legitimacy from scratch.

DAOs are messy. They are inconsistent, occasionally paralytic. But they are also radical. They force us to confront the unvarnished questions: Who defines the mission? What does consent look like when identities are pseudonymous? How are norms enforced when no one can be fired and everyone holds a stake? These are not engineering puzzles; they are cultural ones. A DAO is not simply an organisation—it is a political and philosophical thesis, rendered executable.

Participation itself—proposing, voting, debating, building—is a kind of civic identity work. Members are not mere users; they are partial owners, ideological custodians, and cultural translators. This is why so many DAOs resemble fandoms as much as they resemble corporations. Mascots, memes, rituals, and insider language abound. Votes, emoji reactions, and community calls serve as both decision-making tools and moments of collective theatre. Coordination becomes culture; governance, performance. And out of that performance emerges belonging—portable, opt-in, and often more emotionally binding than traditional affiliations.

All of this points towards a broader shift: the rise of opt-in economies. In the offline world, identity and economic circumstance are largely assigned—by birthplace, by citizenship, by state systems. In the crypto-native sphere, identity is self-assembled. You choose the networks you inhabit, the values you carry, the tokens you stake your time and resources into. Belief is voluntary, and exit is frictionless. This is more than technical novelty—it marks the erosion of "consensus reality," the idea that there is one dominant account of how the world works, replaced instead by overlapping, pluralistic micro-economies.

Viewed this way, crypto is less a financial upheaval than a sociological one. It swaps inherited institutions for constructed ones, national citizenship for tokenised affiliation, and one-way broadcast narratives for memetic coordination. The most enduring protocols are those that answer two questions at once: "What can I earn?" and "What do I believe—and with whom?"

Yet there's a cautionary shadow. The same forces that forge solidarity can breed insularity. The same mechanisms that enable coordination can slide into cultish self-reference. Belief, stripped of self-critique, ossifies into dogma. Decentralisation, worshipped rather than examined, can devolve into an aesthetic rather than a principle. As more people step away from traditional systems into cryptonative ones, the challenge becomes clear: are we building communities of empowerment, or echo chambers of ideological enclosure?

This is the tension under examination. Here, we'll trace how memes operate as both cultural code and financial signal. We'll examine DAOs as laboratories for rethinking human coordination. And we'll consider what it means to inhabit a world where joining a new economy takes no more than a keystroke—where belief can be currency, and community its infrastructure.

Because, in the end, beyond the price charts and the protocol specs, crypto is asking an intensely human question: where do you feel recognised? And who do you trust to build that recognition with you?

Why People Don't Buy Coins—They Join Movements:

To the uninitiated, cryptocurrency appears to be a speculative market populated by technophiles, risk-takers, and opportunists scanning charts and trading tokens. But this interpretation is surface-level. What it misses—fatally—is the emotional engine that powers most crypto adoption: the need to belong. People do not simply buy coins; they enter belief systems. What looks like portfolio diversification is often identity formation in disguise. Investors aren't merely analysing whitepapers or dissecting tokenomics—they're choosing sides, declaring loyalties, and aligning themselves with tribes that offer meaning in a fragmented world. Crypto is less a marketplace than a battlefield of movements, each with its own myths, language, aesthetics, and enemies. And if you don't understand this, you don't understand why people stay, build, or burn out.

The language of the space itself gives it away. People don't talk about "owning" Solana or Bitcoin in the way one owns a bond or a share. They say *I'm in Ethereum. I'm a Bitcoin maxi. We're building on Avalanche.* These are not casual labels. They're shorthand for shared values, collective vision, and ideological stakeholding. A coin, once acquired, quickly becomes a badge. Holding becomes signalling. Speculation becomes narrative participation. This is not unique to crypto—brand affinity, political identification, and sports fandom function similarly—but it is amplified by the economic upside and digital immediacy of blockchain ecosystems. *Belief and investment collapse into one.*

The stakes are heightened by the fact that most of these projects are not finished products but evolving experiments. They need supporters, not just users. Ecosystems survive or wither based not on transaction volumes alone, but on whether a critical mass of people are willing to build, evangelise, troubleshoot, and defend the project in its volatile, formative stages. In this way, a decentralised network resembles a political revolution more than a product launch. It thrives or dies based on whether it can maintain cohesion, morale, and belief across turbulence. The price chart may be the most visible signal, but the social layer beneath it is often the more decisive one.

This is where emotional tribalism comes in. Crypto communities often exhibit the same dynamics found in religious sects, activist movements, or cults. They possess insider jargon, us-versus-them mentalities, purification rituals (airdrop eligibility, staking thresholds), sacred texts (whitepapers), and prophets (founders, influencers). These elements foster cohesion and reinforce a shared sense of destiny—but they also breed echo chambers. *When critique is framed as betrayal and doubt is punished as disloyalty, belief ossifies into dogma.* And that dogma, once calcified, can distort decision-making, inflate perceived threats, and incentivise aggressive self-policing.

It's important, then, to distinguish genuine community from toxic tribalism. The former is generative. It welcomes contribution, rewards critical thought, and adapts to new information. The latter is fragile. It needs enemies to survive, silences dissent, and equates identity with ideology. Healthy crypto communities exhibit resilience through pluralism—they allow disagreement without meltdown. They value robustness over purity. Toxic ones, by contrast, elevate orthodoxy over evidence, clinging to certainty even as data undermines it. They often prioritise narrative control over network health, leading to disillusionment, poor governance, and eventual fragmentation.

One example of this dichotomy is the contrast between early Ethereum and various smaller copycat chains that emerged during the ICO boom. Ethereum's community has endured years of technical setbacks, regulatory scrutiny, and public criticism—not because it promised guaranteed returns, but because it cultivated a builder mindset and intellectual openness. Its forums are filled with debates, not just hype. Its leaders admit mistakes. In contrast, many ICO-era projects surrounded themselves with impermeable hype bubbles, promising moonshots and branding sceptics as FUD-spreaders. The result was predictable: shallow belief collapsed under pressure, and users exited as quickly as they entered.

Understanding these dynamics is essential for any serious crypto participant—not just as a defensive mechanism, but as a diagnostic tool. If you're evaluating a project, don't just study its roadmap or GitHub. Study its Discord. Read the forum debates. Watch how dissent is handled. Are developers transparent or evasive? Are community members curious or combative? Is the culture reflexively bullish or intellectually honest? These signals often reveal more about a project's durability than its market cap or media coverage. *You're not just buying into a token—you're opting into a worldview.*

This is also why memetics matters. Memes are not superficial distractions; they are distilled expressions of group identity. They tell you how a community sees itself, what it mocks, what it aspires to. A meme can often convey more about the emotional DNA of a project than a hundred whitepapers. The Doge meme didn't just make people laugh—it made them feel included. It flipped the seriousness of finance into a game, which in turn attracted a demographic that had felt alienated by institutional jargon and gatekeeping. Shiba Inu followed suit, and while their tokenomics may differ, the underlying mechanism of mass participation through shared humour and irreverence remains the same.

But this memetic power cuts both ways. It can lead to reflexive hostility toward outsiders, especially those perceived as insufficiently committed or ideologically impure. Projects become performance arenas where the loudest supporters police the narrative, often at the expense of nuance and truth. This behaviour is exacerbated by the financial exposure of participants: when your money is tied to your belief system, criticism feels existential. Disagreement becomes a threat, not an invitation to grow. The result is a feedback loop where emotional intensity replaces intellectual clarity.

And yet, the upside of this intensity is not to be dismissed. It is what gives crypto movements their staying power. The very fact that these communities care so deeply—arguably too deeply—is what makes them potent cultural and economic forces. A passionate base, however irrational at times, can bootstrap adoption, amplify innovation, and weather existential threats that would cripple a more tepid user base. This is why movements matter more than markets in early-stage crypto. The best technology doesn't always win—but the best narrative often does.

Still, maturity lies in discernment. Not all movements are worth joining, and not all community enthusiasm is benign. As a thoughtful participant, your responsibility is twofold: first, to assess whether a project's community aligns with your values and intellectual standards; and second, to resist the gravitational pull of groupthink. The ideal investor is not a passive recipient of culture, but an active shaper of it—someone who contributes, questions, and helps nudge the collective toward truth rather than comfort. *Conviction must be earned, not inherited.*

This subchapter asks you to recalibrate your lens. Stop asking only, "What does this token do?" Start asking, "What does this network *believe*?" Who does it include and exclude? What stories does it tell? How does it handle friction, change, uncertainty? The answers to these questions are not peripheral. They are predictive. Because over the long term, projects that cultivate intelligent, adaptable, and self-aware communities will outperform those that rely on hype, purity, and tribal loyalty. What you're investing in is not just code or capital—it's collective character.

When you put money into a coin, you're not just entering a market—you're stepping into a movement. Choose wisely. Because the quality of your returns will often mirror the quality of the crowd you choose to believe with.

Memes as Monetary Infrastructure:

When people think of infrastructure in a monetary context, they picture central banks, payments systems, protocols, and the scaffolding of regulation. They don't usually think of a Shiba Inu meme, a frog on a skateboard, or a crudely rendered cartoon ape. But in the crypto economy—where belief is the binding agent and culture is the carrier—memes are not ornamental. They are foundational. To treat them as trivial is to misunderstand the machinery of value in the digital age. Memes are not mere entertainment—they are consensus algorithms in cultural form. They distil complex ideas into shareable symbols, amplify emotion, encode ideology, and trigger action. In short, *memes are monetary infrastructure*—not because they hold value themselves, but because they channel the social forces that generate and sustain it.

To grasp this, one must first deconstruct the myth that money is purely rational. Traditional economics has long assumed that people make financial decisions based on logic, incentives, and risk-reward analysis. But behavioural finance—and crypto—tell a different story. Emotion, identity, and narrative shape decision-making more than spreadsheets do. Memes operate precisely in this emotional and cognitive layer. They tap into humour, irony, nostalgia, rebellion, and aspiration, often bypassing the rational gatekeepers that might otherwise screen an idea. A meme doesn't persuade you—it *infects* you. And once a meme spreads, it performs the key function of any infrastructure: it standardises belief across a decentralised system.

Consider Dogecoin. Originally created as a parody of crypto speculation, it now has a market capitalisation in the billions. How did that happen? Not through superior technology or institutional partnerships. It happened because a meme—of a bemused Shiba Inu paired with Comic Sans text—became a rallying point for a loosely affiliated community. The meme was accessible, absurd, and inclusive. It mocked the seriousness of finance and welcomed newcomers with irreverence. In doing so, it created a kind of emotional liquidity: people felt safe, amused, seen. That feeling turned into buying, which turned into community, which turned into momentum. Traditional analysts scoffed. But they were using the wrong model. They were measuring infrastructure in code, not culture.

The same principle applies to more 'serious' projects. Ethereum's transition from a technical whitepaper to a cultural movement was lubricated by memes. The "ultrasound money" meme, for example, helped frame Ethereum's deflationary mechanisms in a way that was instantly digestible and emotionally resonant. It wasn't just a supply curve—it was a statement of superiority, an ideological jab at Bitcoin's "sound money" narrative. That meme became shorthand for a host of technical and economic assumptions, enabling evangelists to spread belief at scale without resorting to dense argumentation. The meme didn't explain; it encoded. And that encoding built alignment faster than any whitepaper could.

This is not a new phenomenon. Human societies have always used symbols to organise belief and coordinate behaviour. Flags, religious icons, national anthems—these are all pre-digital memes. They create shared meaning, reduce ambiguity, and foster identity. What is new is the speed and scale at which memes can now propagate, mutate, and monetise. Social media platforms act as accelerants, turning niche jokes into global narratives within hours. And in crypto, where networks are permissionless and liquidity is instant, meme virality translates into market impact almost immediately. *Memes compress the lag between cultural momentum and economic consequence.*

This compression is both powerful and dangerous. On one hand, it allows bottom-up movements to gain traction without institutional endorsement. On the other, it creates susceptibility to hype cycles, manipulation, and herd behaviour. Memes can oversimplify, obscure, and mislead. They can incentivise performative belief rather than informed conviction. Projects can be built on memes that outpace their substance, leading to spectacular rises and equally dramatic collapses. Yet even in these cases, the meme performs a function: it reveals where belief was fragile, where conviction was shallow, and where a narrative was over-leveraged.

The sophistication of meme deployment is evolving. Where early crypto relied on organic, chaotic meme cultures, newer projects often engineer their memes with strategic intent. They hire creative directors, meme consultants, and narrative designers. They launch meme contests, incentivise engagement, and seed Twitter threads with layered references. Memes are no longer afterthoughts—they are front-line tools in community building, brand defence, and protocol differentiation. In some cases, they are even integrated into governance decisions, used to signal consensus or dissent in DAOs. *The meme has become a governance primitive.*

A case in point is the rise of the "gm" meme—short for "good morning"—used across crypto Twitter as a daily ritual of solidarity. What appears trivial is, in fact, profound. The act of tweeting "gm" is a form of signalling: *I'm here. I'm paying attention. I'm part of this.* It costs nothing, carries no information, yet sustains cohesion. It is the simplest possible form of social proof. When markets are volatile and communities are dispersed, such rituals become anchors. They remind participants that they are not alone. The meme is the infrastructure of morale.

But memes don't operate in a vacuum. They require cultural fluency to land. What makes a meme effective in one community may fall flat—or offend—in another. Memes depend on shared reference points, in-jokes, and collective memory. They can build bridges, but they can also draw borders. Memes create in-groups and out-groups. They reward those who get it and exclude those who don't. In this way, memes double as tools of community formation and boundary enforcement. They shape who belongs and who doesn't. And since crypto projects often hinge on community strength, this filtering function becomes strategically significant.

There is also an economic dimension to meme power. Token value is a function of perceived future utility—but also of collective narrative. If a meme can crystallise that narrative in a way that resonates, it can move markets. Traders often speak of sentiment, but sentiment is not a vague mood—it is memetic alignment. The faster a meme captures attention and emotional energy, the faster capital flows. Memes are not just correlated with price movement; they are *causal agents* in the feedback loop of belief and liquidity. This is why meme literacy is no longer optional. It is a critical skill for navigating the modern crypto landscape.

Sceptics may argue that this reduces crypto to theatre. But that critique misses the point. All markets have always been part theatre. The suits, the jargon, the rituals of investor calls and quarterly earnings—they are just more formalised forms of narrative construction. The difference in crypto is transparency and velocity. Memes lay bare what traditional finance hides under layers of decorum: that emotion, identity, and belief are integral to value. That infrastructure is not just technical but cultural. That what people laugh at, share, and repeat is not incidental—it is *instrumental.*

For readers and investors who want to understand where the next wave of value will emerge, the question is not merely, "What is the tech?" It is also, "What is the meme?" What story is being told? Who is telling it? How is it spreading? Does it encode substance or distract from it? These are not aesthetic questions—they are analytical ones. Because in the crypto economy, memes are not post-hoc decorations. They are preconditions for motion.

To navigate this space wisely, one must learn to decode memes not just as jokes, but as economic signals. Not as noise, but as narrative structure. To treat memes as infrastructure is to take seriously the cultural foundations of value—and to recognise that in a world of decentralised networks and permissionless innovation, belief itself must be built, scaled, and maintained. Memes are how we do that. They are not the sideshow. They are the scaffolding.

DAOs and the New Organisational Trust:

Trust has always been the cornerstone of human coordination. Families, firms, governments, religions, and nations have survived or collapsed based not on their resources or ideologies alone, but on the ability to create, scale, and maintain trust across individuals who will never meet. Traditionally, this trust has been intermediated—by executives, judges, auditors, priests, and bureaucrats. What we are now witnessing in the rise of DAOs—Decentralised Autonomous Organisations—is a reengineering of that trust. It is not just a technical upgrade. It is a cultural proposition: that humans can coordinate without central authority, that belief systems can be encoded into protocols, and that legitimacy can be earned without hierarchy.

A DAO is often misunderstood as a "company on the blockchain." This framing is both limiting and misleading. A company has a CEO. A DAO does not. A company relies on contracts enforced by courts. A DAO relies on smart contracts enforced by code. A company optimises for shareholder value. A DAO may optimise for community health, artistic experimentation, climate impact, or anything else it explicitly defines. What makes a DAO novel is not the assets it holds or the functions it performs—it is *how decisions are made* and *who participates in making them.* Power in a DAO is distributed, not delegated. That distribution is not incidental—it is structural.

To understand the radicalism of DAOs, consider the historical progression of organisational trust. In agrarian societies, trust was local and face-to-face. In the industrial age, it scaled through bureaucracy and branding. In the digital age, it began to scale through platforms—but platforms remained centralised gatekeepers. Facebook coordinates billions, but its rules are set unilaterally. Google organises the world's information, but edits its algorithm in private. These models scale efficiency, not democracy. DAOs propose something different: *a protocol-native model of coordination*, where governance is transparent, rules are programmable, and participation is permissionless.

Take MakerDAO, one of the earliest and most influential DAOs in the crypto ecosystem. It governs the DAI stablecoin, a decentralised currency pegged to the US dollar but not issued by a central bank. Its governance token, MKR, allows holders to vote on protocol parameters—from collateral types to interest rates. Proposals are posted publicly. Debates happen in forums. Code changes are visible. This structure is not a utopia—it is noisy, slow, and sometimes fractious. But it is *legible*. That legibility is a form of accountability. It contrasts starkly with the opaque decision-making of both traditional finance and tech conglomerates.

Critically, DAOs decouple trust from identity. In conventional organisations, power accrues through credentials, titles, or insider networks. In a DAO, influence is earned through participation, contribution, and sometimes token ownership. One might be pseudonymous yet respected, anonymous yet impactful. This opens the door to a more meritocratic logic—but also raises difficult questions about representation, inequality, and sybil resistance. If anyone can vote, how do you prevent manipulation? If tokens grant votes, does wealth override wisdom? These tensions are not bugs—they are design parameters. DAOs force us to confront them explicitly.

The design space of DAOs is still embryonic. Some are minimal—just multisig wallets coordinating grant funding. Others are baroque—sprawling networks of working groups, community calls, reputation systems, and on-chain governance modules. What unites them is not form but *philosophy*. DAOs embody a belief in bottom-up coordination, in transparency over opacity, and in programmable trust over interpersonal trust. They attract people not just with economic incentives but with ideological alignment. Joining a DAO is not just buying into a project—it is opting into a governance paradigm.

Yet the promise of DAOs must be weighed against their limitations. They can be slow to act, vulnerable to apathy, and difficult to scale. Consensus is hard. Voter turnout is low. Strategic coherence can be elusive. Critics point out that many DAOs suffer from token plutocracy—where large holders wield disproportionate influence. Others drift into dysfunction, unable to make timely decisions or resolve internal disputes. But these failures do not negate the model. They signal a deeper truth: *trust is easy to centralise, hard to distribute.* The value of DAOs lies not in flawless execution but in the experimentation they enable.

One of the most revealing aspects of DAOs is how they blend software engineering with social engineering. A DAO is both a governance protocol and a belief system. It must inspire participation, maintain alignment, and evolve with its community. This requires not just code but culture. Successful DAOs often invest heavily in onboarding rituals, shared memes, contributor journeys, and community storytelling. These are not soft add-ons. They are mechanisms of cohesion. They create continuity in a structure that lacks hierarchy. They help answer a core question: *Why should anyone care enough to contribute?*

BanklessDAO, for instance, has grown into a vibrant ecosystem of media, education, and tooling—all coordinated through a network of contributors with no central management. Its success is not due to a killer app but to a shared ethos: that people should have sovereignty over their financial lives. That ethos is sustained through weekly calls, editorial guidelines, token incentives, and cultural narratives. The infrastructure is visible; the belief is palpable. Together, they form a new kind of organisational trust—*not trust in a person or brand, but in a collectively maintained system of intent.*

This reframes how we think about institutions. Traditionally, institutions derive legitimacy from history, expertise, or legal authority. DAOs derive legitimacy from transparency, participation, and coherence. Their authority is not bestowed—it is earned, and continually renegotiated. This makes them fragile, but also adaptable. They can fork. They can evolve. They can die and be reborn. They operate more like biological systems than legal entities. And like all organisms, their survival depends on their ability to sustain internal alignment while adapting to external change.

DAOs are also testing grounds for political theory. They revisit ancient debates about direct democracy versus delegated governance, about majority rule versus minority rights, about the role of incentives versus norms. Some DAOs experiment with quadratic voting to reduce plutocracy. Others explore reputation-weighted voting to privilege long-term contributors. Still others use rotating councils, delegated committees, or consensus thresholds. The experiments are messy—but deeply instructive. *DAOs are political laboratories masked as software projects.*

This is why DAOs matter beyond crypto. They hint at new models for civic engagement, organisational design, and even international cooperation. Imagine a climate DAO coordinating reforestation through global contributors. A media DAO funding investigative journalism. A science DAO incentivising open research. These are not distant fantasies—they already exist in early form. The challenge is not technological. It is cultural and operational. *Can we sustain belief without a central priesthood? Can we coordinate action without a boss?*

These are profound questions—and DAOs are how we prototype answers. Not every DAO will succeed. Many will fail. But what they leave behind is a deeper understanding of what trust looks like when unbundled from institutions, when reassembled from the ground up, when mediated by code rather than charisma. In doing so, they offer a glimpse of coordination beyond coercion, of governance beyond gatekeepers, of belief systems that are not inherited but chosen.

To participate in or even observe a DAO is to witness the messy birth of a new organisational logic. It is not clean or finished. But it is alive, dynamic, and revealing. For those trying to understand where society might be headed—not just technologically, but philosophically—DAOs are not peripheral. They are front and centre. They show us that trust need not be vertical to be real, and that coordination need not be centralised to be powerful.

Opt-In Economies and the Death of Consensus Reality:

For most of human history, the economy has been treated as a shared reality—one defined by borders, institutions, and national currencies. A farmer in 18th-century France and a banker in 20th-century London may have lived in wildly different material circumstances, but they were bound to the same idea: that the economy is a fixed environment, like gravity, that one must adapt to. The premise was simple. Whether you were a monarchist or a Marxist, you had no option but to play within the rules of the system. What crypto introduces—quietly at first, then increasingly provocatively—is the concept that one can *opt out.* Not by withdrawing from modern life, but by participating in new systems entirely. Not just new currencies, but new economic logics. *Crypto is not simply about creating money; it is about creating alternative economic realities.*

To understand the radicalism of this shift, we must first recognise how deeply "consensus reality" is embedded in the economic order. Consensus reality is what happens when most people agree—implicitly or explicitly—on how value is created, stored, and exchanged. It is what makes national currencies viable, stock markets functional, and legal contracts enforceable. Fiat money works not because it is backed by gold or math, but because it is backed by collective belief and state enforcement. Central banks maintain price stability not through universal truth, but through policy consensus. When you swipe your credit card, dozens of financial entities—from banks to clearing houses—participate in an orchestration built entirely on trust in the system. That trust is invisible but totalising. It defines who gets to participate, under what conditions, and with what stakes.

Crypto fractures this consensus. It doesn't just critique the system; it offers working alternatives. When someone buys ether and starts transacting on the Ethereum network, they are not merely speculating—they are migrating. They are aligning with a different set of assumptions about authority, ownership, and value creation. They are saying: I trust cryptographic consensus over central bank policy. I prefer code-based enforcement to legal adjudication. I believe in economic rules that are transparent, decentralised, and borderless. This is not just a change of tools—it is a change of *ontology*. Crypto introduces the idea that multiple economic realities can coexist, and that individuals can *choose* which one to live inside.

This opt-in quality is what makes crypto powerful—and culturally destabilising. Traditional economies are defined territorially. You are born into a monetary system, pay taxes in its currency, and are subject to its monetary policy whether you agree or not. With crypto, geography becomes less relevant. Economic affiliation becomes more like ideological alignment. You can be physically located in Lagos but financially native to Bitcoin. You can live in Berlin but participate primarily in the Solana ecosystem. You can be a Filipino gamer earning income in Axie Infinity's token economy. These are not speculative hypotheticals—they are happening now, and at scale.

The implications are profound. Crypto challenges the monopoly that nation-states have held over economic infrastructure. It erodes the default assumption that a single system must govern everyone. It introduces plurality where there used to be uniformity. And it forces us to confront the cultural consequences of this pluralism. If people increasingly live in economic systems of their own choosing, what happens to shared narratives? What happens to policy consensus? What happens to collective responsibility?

Consider the rise of play-to-earn ecosystems such as Axie Infinity, or more broadly, the gig economies being constructed on blockchain platforms. These systems allow users to earn tokens through participation—gaming, content creation, governance activity—and to convert that income into fiat currencies, stablecoins, or goods and services. On the surface, these look like new forms of work. But on a deeper level, they represent exits from traditional labour markets and income models. They decouple earning from formal employment. They invite people to *generate value under new rules*, with new currencies, and for new audiences. This is not just a change in compensation. It is a change in *what is considered economically legitimate.*

A similar dynamic unfolds with decentralised finance (DeFi). When users lend, borrow, or trade on DeFi protocols, they are not interfacing with banks—they are interacting with autonomous code. There is no central counterparty, no compliance department, no call centre. Value flows through permissionless smart contracts. Access is determined not by credit score or citizenship, but by internet connection and wallet address. In opting into DeFi, users are not just seeking better yield—they are affirming a different philosophy of access and trust. *They are choosing algorithmic trust over institutional trust.*

This leads to cultural frictions that are as significant as the technical breakthroughs. If one group believes in fiat currencies managed by democratically accountable institutions, and another believes in algorithmically capped token supplies with no central control, they are not just disagreeing on policy—they are operating from different epistemologies. They value different things, trust different mechanisms, and define risk differently. This is the death of consensus reality—not because one system wins over the other, but because multiple systems now exist in parallel, and no central authority can enforce a singular narrative.

There are both liberating and destabilising consequences to this shift. On the liberating side, marginalised communities can create economic systems that reflect their values, priorities, and needs. Artists can mint their own currencies. Activists can build fundraising DAOs outside of NGO gatekeeping. Developers can create governance structures that reward participation rather than credentialism. These are not just financial innovations—they are *sovereign experiments*. They reflect a reassertion of agency in a world where many feel structurally excluded.

But there is a darker dimension too. When people exit consensus reality, they may also exit shared responsibility. If your economic system is bounded by your Discord server or DAO membership, what obligation do you have to broader society? If wealth is denominated in tokens that outsiders don't understand or accept, how do we discuss inequality? If inflation in a national economy is irrelevant to your token-denominated wealth, does civic engagement degrade? These are not abstract concerns. They raise urgent questions about social cohesion, legitimacy, and accountability.

Moreover, not all opt-in economies are healthy. Some are built on speculative mania, cult dynamics, or misinformation. They may foster insular echo chambers where questioning the narrative is seen as betrayal. They may reward early adopters at the expense of newcomers. They may collapse under governance failures or tokenomics that were never designed for sustainability. In a world of opt-in economies, *due diligence is not just a financial skill—it is a civic one.*

This is why understanding the architecture of these new systems is critical. Who controls the protocol? How are decisions made? What is the incentive structure? What happens when something breaks? These questions are often more important than price charts or roadmaps. They determine whether a given system is a playground, a Ponzi, a proto-nation, or something in between. They also help us understand the *psychological dimension* of opting in. People don't just join because the yield is good. They join because the system reflects something they believe—or want to believe—about the world.

Crypto does not promise utopia. It offers *optionality*. The ability to choose which rules to play by, which authorities to trust, and which economic logic to inhabit. That optionality is intoxicating—but it also fragments our collective sense of economic "truth." This is not inherently bad. Every major technological shift has challenged dominant paradigms. The printing press shattered the monopoly of religious authority. The internet fragmented media consensus. Crypto is now doing the same to economic authority. Whether we see that as liberation or risk depends on how we manage the transition—and how well we understand what is being unbundled.

At its core, crypto is not just a financial revolution. It is a cultural experiment in self-determination. Opt-in economies allow us to ask: What if value were defined not by tradition or central decree, but by choice, alignment, and voluntary participation? What if we could build economic systems that reflect our deepest values rather than inherited assumptions? What if money, trust, and coordination could be reimagined from first principles?

The answers are still unfolding. But the questions are already changing how we think about systems, sovereignty, and society itself. Crypto didn't just introduce new assets—it introduced a new *architecture of belief*. And once that door has been opened, it is difficult—perhaps impossible—to close.

Chapter 5
Risk as a Mirror – What Volatility Reveals

Volatility, in the neat language of finance, is meant to be a number—a tidy calculation of how widely returns scatter over a given stretch of time. On paper, it is cool, clean, objective. But anyone who has felt it in the gut knows it is nothing of the sort. It is raw. It is intimate. It tugs at your doubts, swells your pride, and quietly exposes the wiring of your character. In markets, as in the rest of life, risk is never just something you handle—it is something that lays you bare. Here, we look at volatility not as a cold statistical curve, but as a kind of psychological forge. If you want to know yourself with any honesty, watch how you behave when the ground shifts.

In crypto, this self-confrontation is impossible to sidestep. Traditional markets still keep to a civilised schedule, buffered by regulation, trading hours, and layers of protocol. Crypto has none of that. It never closes. No gatekeepers, no handholding, no pause for breath—just you, a wallet, a glowing screen, and numbers flickering without mercy, day and night. In such an arena, each price tick feels personal. A sudden drop can sting like a public slight; a soaring rally can feel like the world nodding in approval. The chart is no longer just market data—it becomes a running verdict on your wit, timing, and very sense of self. The swings test more than your capital; they test your ego.

This is why conversations about crypto so often turn to feelings. Excitement, panic, envy, pride, shame—they are not side effects; they are the experience. Few investors lie awake at night fretting over the finer points of Ethereum's next network upgrade. They lie awake because they feel exposed. Because they think they've misread the room, missed their moment, or hitched their identity to a market that neither knows nor cares who they are. Crypto investing is theatre in real time, with risk and belief as the leading roles. And often, the most unstable element in the plot isn't the coin—it's the investor's own mind.

From this flows one of crypto's most persistent mental traps: the "I should have bought" refrain. It exists in all markets, but crypto supercharges it. You imagine your life had you bought Bitcoin in 2012, Ethereum in 2016, or Solana before its meteoric climb. It's a seductive daydream—part spreadsheet, part personal indictment. It is not only about missed profit; it is about the sting of hindsight, the suspicion that you failed to act when you should have, that you have been here before, in markets and in life, and hesitated.

This loop is fuelled by hindsight bias, that tidy fiction that the past was always obvious. It tells you your inaction was negligence, erasing the uncertainty you actually faced at the time. The trouble with this is twofold: it robs you of courage for the future, and it warps your sense of luck into a moral scorecard. The truth is, investing—especially in new frontiers like crypto—is not fortune-telling. It is the art of building convictions strong enough to act under fog. In this light, forgiveness of one's past self is not soft sentiment; it's strategic maintenance.

The aim, then, is not to strip emotion out of investing—that's both impossible and, frankly, undesirable. It's to sift it. Some feelings carry signal; others carry sabotage. Regret can sharpen your process if you let it. Left unchecked, it turns to cynicism. Pride can validate your judgment, but if it blinds you to fresh evidence, it becomes a liability. Even fear is useful, provided it's tempered by nerve. Mastery lies not in detachment, but in tuned awareness—the ability to register your inner weather without being swept away by it.

This is where the idea of "practising volatility" earns its keep. We tend to think of risk tolerance as a trait—like eye colour—fixed for life. But in reality, it's a muscle. You can strengthen it, through deliberate exposure and reflection. Just as training the body means controlled strain to build capacity, training the psyche can mean taking measured risks to expand emotional bandwidth. This is not about reckless punts in the name of hardening up. It's about using the churn of the market as a workout in reading—and recalibrating—your own responses.

Say your portfolio drops by 10%. Don't just check the figures; take note of the stories that leap to mind. Are you jumping to catastrophe? Treating a dip as a verdict on your intelligence? Blurring the line between price and self-worth? These are diagnostic cues. The market is not a mentor, but it is a relentless feedback loop—one that will present the same test again and again until you either adapt or exit.

The same lens applies to gains. If a token doubles overnight, what's the script in your head? That you're sharp enough to see what others missed? That your instincts are flawless? Tempting narratives, but they inflate the ego like hidden leverage. And as with leverage, the comedown can be brutal. In crypto, the ego is often the real margin call—your assets may survive a crash, but your judgment might not.

Seen from this angle, the richest return on crypto investing isn't necessarily measured in currency. It's the chance to witness yourself in the presence of risk—to observe what you believe about the market, and what you believe about you. Are you adventurous, or simply restless? Cautious, or afraid of being wrong? Do you crave profit as proof, or freedom from needing proof at all?

Such questions shift you from automatic reaction to intentional choice. They break the habit of letting your mood rise and fall with the candlesticks. They help you distinguish between a passing squall and a lasting storm. And they cultivate what might be the rarest quality in an investor: equanimity. Not the numbness of apathy, but the steadiness of composure. Not withdrawal from risk, but an unshaken seat within it.

Crypto will not stop convulsing. It will lurch, spike, tumble, and mystify. This is not a design flaw—it is part of its youthful energy and experimental nature. But if we can treat each bout of turbulence as a lesson rather than an attack, we end up learning something larger than market mechanics. Because risk is everywhere: in ventures, in relationships, in ambitions that stretch us. The way we navigate it in crypto is often a microcosm of how we navigate it everywhere else.

So this is not a manual for hedging strategies. It is a prompt to turn inward. To map the interplay between your portfolio and your personality. To build frameworks not just for enduring volatility, but for being shaped, in the right ways, by it. If you can see yourself clearly in crypto's storm, you are not merely honing your craft as an investor—you are growing into a more deliberate, more awake version of yourself.

The Emotional Tax of Uncertainty:

The most taxing part of investing in crypto isn't the risk of loss—it's the weight of *not knowing*. It's the psychological cost of uncertainty, the hourly ambush of "what if" scenarios that cloud judgement and fray attention. The screen may show you a numerical dip or spike, but your nervous system registers something far more personal: ambiguity, threat, and self-doubt. This constant exposure to unpredictability is not just a financial challenge—it is a cognitive and emotional toll that, left unmanaged, can degrade decision-making, erode self-trust, and quietly distort your sense of stability. *Uncertainty, when left unexamined, becomes a form of psychological drag—unseen, but heavy.*

Crypto magnifies this dynamic uniquely. Unlike traditional financial markets with structured disclosure schedules, guarded institutional rhythms, and regulated downtime, the crypto ecosystem is perpetually open, aggressively decentralised, and fuelled by rumour as much as research. Prices shift while you sleep. Narratives invert within days. Technological breakthroughs coexist with rug pulls. A single tweet can devalue months of conviction. The market is not simply volatile—it is narratively unstable. You are not reacting only to numbers, but to an unending stream of noise, contradiction, and emotional contagion. *In this environment, the uncertainty is not merely about outcomes—it's existential.* What is real? Who can be trusted? What matters next?

The psychological tax of this instability is rarely acknowledged in mainstream financial discourse. It hides behind terms like "risk appetite" or "market temperament", as though it were a matter of character rather than cognition. But uncertainty isn't just an abstract backdrop—it's a neurological stressor. Cognitive science has long shown that uncertainty activates similar neural circuits as physical pain. The human brain evolved to reduce ambiguity quickly and decisively, often at the cost of nuance. When faced with unpredictable inputs, our minds rush to premature conclusions just to regain a sense of control. *This is why, under sustained market stress, otherwise rational investors can become reactive, tribal, or oddly compulsive.*

One of the most corrosive symptoms of chronic exposure to uncertainty is narrative overcommitment. Faced with shifting signals, many investors cling to a single explanatory framework—whether bullish optimism, deep cynicism, or conspiratorial mistrust—because it provides emotional refuge. This isn't a flaw in intelligence; it's a defensive strategy. Certainty, even if false, is neurologically easier to carry than ambiguity. But the cost is subtle: intellectual rigidity, confirmation bias, and the inability to adapt. In a space like crypto—where technological evolution, regulatory change, and cultural dynamics converge—this rigidity is fatal to clarity.

The antidote is not detachment in the cold, stoic sense, but *a disciplined form of emotional decentralisation.* That is, the ability to hold your identity separate from market performance, your belief systems separate from current price action, and your emotional centre of gravity separate from external chaos. This is not emotional numbness. On the contrary, it requires a high degree of emotional awareness. Detachment here means not *feeling less*, but *reacting with discernment.* You can observe a 30% drop without tying it to your worth. You can track a mooning token without presuming omniscience. You can watch without becoming swallowed.

To develop this posture, one must first stop expecting clarity. Much of the psychological pain of uncertainty comes not from ambiguity itself, but from the internal demand that ambiguity be resolved. Investors tell themselves they must know what's next, must find the hidden signal, must decode the right thread before the window closes. But this urgency is often misdirected. It chases resolution at the expense of understanding. It rewards speed over thoughtfulness. And it depletes the emotional stamina required for long-term conviction. *By learning to sit with uncertainty, rather than eliminate it, you begin to reduce its psychological toll.*

This approach requires replacing the default mindset of prediction with a mindset of scenario preparedness. Instead of asking "What will happen?", ask "What might plausibly happen—and how will I respond?" This subtle shift removes the emotional pressure to be right and replaces it with the practical discipline of readiness. You move from ego-centric forecasting to systems thinking. You begin to build internal protocols, much like resilient code in a decentralised system. You stop trying to beat the market at its own game and start shaping your own mental architecture to survive and thrive within it.

But building this kind of resilience also demands lifestyle calibration. The emotional cost of uncertainty compounds under certain conditions: sleep deprivation, overexposure to digital noise, lack of physical movement, isolation from real conversations. These are not wellness clichés—they are core inputs to cognitive clarity. An investor who compulsively refreshes prices every fifteen minutes, isolates from divergent viewpoints, and substitutes digital dopamine for physical grounding will not make better decisions over time. They will burn out—slowly, then all at once. *Your psychological inputs are part of your portfolio—neglect them and your returns will reflect it.*

It's also essential to recognise that emotional detachment is not evenly distributed across all types of uncertainty. Some investors may weather price fluctuations with grace, but crumble when regulatory ambiguity strikes. Others may tolerate macroeconomic shocks but become anxious over community drama or token politics. Understanding your *personal uncertainty profile*—the kinds of ambiguity that trigger you most—is key to designing effective strategies for emotional containment. This isn't just about self-awareness. It's about reducing behavioural leakage: the unconscious ways your emotions distort your investing edge.

Another overlooked practice is scheduled disengagement. In an always-on market, where opportunity is presumed to hide in every second, the fear of missing out becomes a form of psychological tyranny. Investors find it hard to step away—not because they are greedy, but because they are afraid of being caught off guard. But sustained presence in a volatile space creates diminishing clarity. Much like a muscle that fatigues from constant use, the emotional faculty for discernment weakens without recovery. Building deliberate windows of disengagement—time without market exposure, signal-checking, or strategy tweaking—is not a luxury. It is a maintenance protocol.

This emotional architecture is not about becoming robotic. It's about *learning to co-exist with uncertainty without surrendering to it.* True detachment allows for fluid engagement: you can enter the market with clear eyes, absorb volatility without reactivity, and exit your screen without existential dread. You can remain curious without being destabilised, informed without being inflamed. This doesn't make you immune to losses, but it makes you less vulnerable to the *secondary losses*—the ones that come from poor decisions made in emotionally saturated states.

Lastly, it's important to anchor your practice in a framework of internal metrics. If your sense of success is tied only to external results—price, ROI, short-term trends—your emotional balance will always be hostage to forces you cannot control. But if you define your progress through internal signals—how clearly you executed your strategy, how well you managed your attention, how skillfully you responded to surprise—then uncertainty becomes data rather than danger. It becomes something to work with, not against. *Your composure becomes the real edge.*

Crypto will not get less volatile. The nature of innovation, decentralisation, and speculation guarantees that uncertainty is baked into the system. But our response to it need not be anxious, reactive, or exhausting. With thoughtful emotional architecture, disciplined attention hygiene, and a redefined relationship to ambiguity, we can reduce the hidden tax that uncertainty extracts from our mental reserves. The reward is not just more effective investing—it is a clearer, calmer, more resilient self. One that no longer needs the world to be certain in order to move forward with purpose.

Ego in the Ledger:

There is no line item for ego on a trading screen, no ticker symbol that reflects self-worth, no dashboard that warns when identity is becoming entangled with outcome. Yet for many investors—especially in crypto—*the most volatile asset is not Bitcoin or Solana; it's the sense of self riding behind each trade.* Every chart becomes a mirror. Every gain affirms personal foresight. Every loss risks puncturing not just wealth, but the narrative of who we believe we are. In the decentralised economy, where the rules are few and the risks are many, investing ceases to be a purely financial act. It becomes an emotional audition for competence, foresight, and status.

This is not a trivial or abstract concern. Investing, particularly in emerging, decentralised systems, confronts us with fundamental psychological questions: How much control do I believe I have over the future? What does success look like on *my* terms? And most uncomfortably, what do I think it says about me if I'm wrong? These aren't just personal quirks. They're identity narratives—often implicit, often inherited—that drive behaviour more than any technical analysis ever could. When a token surges or collapses, we're not just updating spreadsheets; we're renegotiating the stories we tell ourselves about our judgement, agency, and worth.

The financial self is, in many ways, a construct. It's not just the aggregation of your net worth—it's how your psyche processes your relationship with risk, reward, and reputation. For many, especially first-time investors in highly public spaces like crypto, the act of investing becomes performative. Screenshots of gains, ideological convictions on-chain, alignment with maximalist communities—these are not simply expressions of interest. They are attempts to craft a legible identity in a market that rewards narrative just as much as numerical return. *Profit becomes proof not only of timing, but of personhood.* To be right is to be relevant. To be early is to be seen.

The danger, however, is that identity attachment breeds fragility. When financial performance is fused with ego, volatility becomes existential. A dip in the market feels like a personal rebuke. A missed entry point stirs disproportionate regret. An alternative thesis outperforming your own invites defensiveness. This psychological entanglement leads to what behavioural finance calls "identity-driven risk"—the distortion of decision-making to protect the self-image rather than optimise for outcome. It is not loss aversion, per se, but *ego preservation.* Investors hold losing positions too long because selling would mean admitting error. They double down not out of conviction, but because retreat would rupture their internal narrative of intelligence and foresight.

This is where traditional finance often fails to prepare us for the emotional complexity of decentralised systems. In classical models, investors are presumed to be rational agents maximising utility. But the crypto space is not populated by economic robots—it's a theatre of belief, speculation, and status-seeking. The permissionless nature of blockchain means anyone can participate, but also that anyone can *watch*. Public wallets, open-source strategies, Discord calls—these create a visibility that subtly shifts incentives from outcome optimisation to image curation. *You're no longer just investing; you're broadcasting.* And when the audience is global, the stakes are not just monetary. They are reputational.

This is particularly relevant in an ecosystem where meritocracy is often assumed, but rarely interrogated. Crypto culture frequently champions the myth of the sovereign individual—the self-educated, independent thinker who "made it" through insight and conviction. While this ethos has its virtues, it also reinforces a psychological rigidity. If success is presumed to be purely merit-based, then failure must be personal. There is little room for luck, structural privilege, or external complexity in the crypto success story. And so, when things go wrong—as they inevitably do—many investors turn inward with shame or outward with blame, rather than engaging in sober, systemic analysis. *Ego makes it hard to learn.*

To invest with clarity, then, requires developing what might be called *ego literacy*—an awareness of how your self-image is influencing your perception of data, risk, and narrative. Are you doubling down on a token because you truly believe in its fundamentals, or because admitting you're wrong would threaten your standing in a Telegram group? Are you resisting a shift in your thesis because of intellectual integrity, or because you've publicly aligned your identity with a particular ideology? These are not easy questions. But they are the ones that separate adaptive investors from ideological martyrs.

One powerful exercise is to audit your self-talk during market movement. When prices surge, what inner commentary arises? Is it "I knew it—I'm smart"? When prices fall, is it "I always mess this up"? Both responses signal ego entanglement. In a healthy investing posture, gains and losses are seen as data—inputs to refine, not verdicts on identity. This doesn't mean becoming cold or clinical. It means holding your self-worth as something independent of external outcomes. *The market is not your judge—it is your feedback loop.*

It also helps to create intentional psychological boundaries between the role of investor and the role of self. Just as a professional athlete learns to separate performance from personhood, a disciplined investor must learn to hold their market persona lightly. This can be done through journaling practices that distinguish *what you did* from *why you did it.* It can also be reinforced through community environments that reward reflection over bravado, humility over hype. The healthiest investment communities are not echo chambers of profit screenshots; they are forums where doubt, loss, and learning are normalised. Where ego isn't erased, but *contextualised.*

Another overlooked aspect of ego in investing is *time preference.* Investors with fragile egos often chase short-term wins—not because they need liquidity, but because they crave proof. They need the market to affirm their intelligence quickly and often. This leads to overtrading, emotional whiplash, and burnout. Long-term thinking, by contrast, requires a stable ego. It asks you to delay gratification, to tolerate being temporarily wrong in service of deeper accuracy, and to invest without constant applause. The most successful investors aren't always the smartest—they are the ones most capable of detaching their self-image from their scorecard. *They know who they are, regardless of what the market says today.*

All of this is intensified in a digital culture where virality can confer status faster than actual value creation. Memecoins, influencer endorsements, and performative conviction often outpace real insight. This distorts the feedback loops investors rely on, making it harder to separate what is *popular* from what is *true.* When everyone around you is shouting certainty, it can feel like humility is weakness. But the opposite is true. In a noisy market, quiet self-assurance is a form of alpha. You don't have to be louder—you have to be clearer. And clarity begins where ego ends.

There is no way to completely remove ego from investing. Nor would that be desirable. Ego, in its healthy form, provides motivation, courage, and a sense of stake. The goal is not to eliminate it, but to *integrate* it—so that it serves your strategy rather than hijacking it. This requires daily practice, brutal honesty, and psychological hygiene. It means asking not just "What am I buying?" but "What part of me is buying this?" It means recognising that the most powerful ledger you manage is not on-chain—it's the internal account of how you see yourself, and whether that self can remain steady when everything else is swinging.

By building ego awareness into your investment process, you become harder to manipulate, more adaptive under pressure, and more grounded in your decision-making. You stop outsourcing your confidence to price charts. You stop needing the market to tell you who you are. And from that posture, paradoxically, you often perform better—because you can see more clearly, act more patiently, and endure more honestly. Investing, then, is not just a technical game. It is an identity laboratory. And every trade, every thesis, every moment of doubt is a chance to refine not just your portfolio—but your self.

The "I Should've Bought" Syndrome:

Few phrases are more universal—or more psychologically corrosive—than "I should've bought." It's whispered in Telegram threads, muttered under breath at news headlines, and etched into the internal monologue of almost every investor who has watched a digital asset they once ignored explode in value. The words carry the weight of lost opportunity, the sting of hindsight, and the illusion that a different version of you—smarter, faster, braver—might now be rich. But beneath this seemingly casual lament lies a deep tangle of cognitive bias, identity conflict, and emotional miscalibration. *Regret is not just a feeling; it's a belief system about what could have been, rooted in distorted memory and overestimated foresight.*

The "I should've bought" syndrome is a particularly acute pathology in crypto markets because of their visibility, volatility, and velocity. In traditional markets, missing a trade often fades quietly. In crypto, it haunts you with memes, charts, and Twitter threads that amplify your missed timing into public narrative. The token you dismissed at $12 is now at $1,200, and every mention of it reminds you—not just of the money you didn't make—but of the self you didn't become. This is where regret becomes more than just a passing emotional wave. *It becomes a lens through which you reinterpret your entire decision-making history, often unfairly.*

The mechanics of this bias are well studied. Hindsight bias—the tendency to see past events as having been more predictable than they actually were—is central to the syndrome. After an asset appreciates, the mind conveniently forgets the uncertainty, confusion, or skepticism that was present when the decision was first considered. Instead, it reconstructs the past as if the outcome was obvious, even inevitable. "It was so clear," you tell yourself. "All the signs were there." But this is a psychological illusion. *Clarity is a privilege granted only by time.* What feels like failure of insight is often just the natural by-product of incomplete information, prudence, or competing priorities.

To break free from this mental trap, the first step is to recognise that you're not regretting a decision. You're regretting a fantasy. The regret is rarely about not owning a coin—it's about not being who you believe you would've become had you made the perfect move. The mind quickly extrapolates from a missed purchase to an alternate identity: the version of you who is now financially free, publicly admired, and retrospectively validated. *It's not just money you think you've lost—it's a narrative arc in which you were the hero.* But that story is fiction. You don't know if you would have held the asset, or sold too early, or bought the next wrong thing with false confidence. Counterfactual fantasies are always clean because they skip the messy realities of actual participation.

Moreover, this syndrome thrives in ecosystems where performance is hyper-visible. Crypto platforms are drenched in screenshots of gains, celebratory posts, and shaming memes about being "late." Social comparison, already a powerful psychological force, becomes relentless when every moment online reminds you that others moved faster or believed more. This environment creates a subtle but dangerous equation: *price action = personal validation.* You begin to judge your insight not by its logic, but by its proximity to profit. And when others succeed visibly, their gains become, irrationally, your losses. Their wins are treated as your missed shots. But this is a false accounting. *Someone else's windfall says nothing about your mistake unless your process was flawed—and that's a different inquiry entirely.*

That distinction—between outcome and process—is critical. Smart investors do not judge themselves purely on results. They evaluate the quality of their reasoning at the time of decision. Did you pass on a token because you had incomplete data? Because you didn't understand the protocol? Because the tokenomics looked unsound? These are not failures—they are signs of discipline. The fact that an asset appreciated doesn't invalidate your original caution. In fact, resisting impulsive entry is often the mark of maturity. *Markets can be irrational longer than your conviction can stay solvent.* The test of a good investor is not omniscience; it's process integrity under uncertainty.

That said, unchecked regret is corrosive. It erodes confidence, clouds current judgement, and fosters a cycle of reactive behaviour. Investors who internalise "I should've bought" too deeply often swing to overcompensation—chasing pumps, aping trends, or abandoning thesis discipline in an attempt to "make up for lost time." But the market is indifferent to your emotional repair. It rewards clarity, not desperation. When you treat the past as debt, you distort the future. The antidote is not to suppress regret, but to *digest it deliberately*. Regret is a data point, not a destiny.

This is where the practice of *self-forgiveness* enters as a strategic skill, not just a moral virtue. It begins with acknowledging the counterfactual narrative as just that—a narrative. You are not the person you imagine in your imagined win. You are the person you actually are, and you acted based on what you knew at the time. Forgiveness does not mean ignoring poor decisions. It means evaluating them proportionately. Did you act out of fear, ignorance, bias? Fine—own that. But don't condemn your entire investing identity for a single omission. *You're allowed to learn without self-punishment.* Growth is not a straight line—it's a series of recalibrated errors.

One helpful tool is a *missed-opportunity journal.* This is not for wallowing, but for analysis. Write down the asset, the decision you made, the reasoning at the time, and the factors you now believe were missing or misweighted. Then log what you learned. Over time, you will notice patterns—not just in the assets you miss, but in how your psychological architecture responds to them. Maybe you chronically underrate meme assets, or overweigh founder charisma, or avoid entry after a single red candle. These are not character flaws—they are cognitive habits. By making them visible, you regain agency.

Perspective also matters. Zooming out, every investor misses something monumental. No one has perfect exposure. Warren Buffett famously missed tech stocks in the 1990s. Prominent crypto traders missed Bitcoin in 2011. The key is not to avoid all mistakes—it's to avoid the ones that compromise your ability to keep learning. *The most dangerous regret is not missing an asset. It's missing the chance to get better.* And you cannot improve if you're stuck in a cycle of shame.

Perhaps most importantly, don't outsource your validation to the price chart. Crypto markets are volatile, meme-driven, and deeply reflexive. What works today may not work tomorrow. The same token that pumped 10x could crash 90% next quarter. If your confidence rides entirely on being "early," you've built your identity on sand. Real conviction is not about timing the bottom. It's about *understanding why you're participating at all.* Are you here for speculation, for ideology, for technology, for career? Clarity on this anchors your perspective. It allows you to say, "Yes, I missed that pump. But I'm still on my path." That kind of internal orientation immunises you from chasing ghosts.

Ultimately, "I should've bought" is not just a statement about a missed trade. It's a test of psychological resilience, epistemic humility, and narrative discipline. The market will always offer a next thing. Your job is not to catch everything. Your job is to build a worldview sturdy enough to survive missing a few things along the way. That requires letting go of fantasy, forgiving the self, refining the process, and staying emotionally available to the next opportunity. Because the real tragedy is not that you missed a 100x coin. *It's that you let one missed shot keep you from ever shooting again.*

Practicing Volatility:

Volatility is not the exception in crypto markets—it is the terrain. Every investor knows this intellectually, but far fewer are prepared for the visceral, psychological, and behavioural demands that come with actually enduring it. Watching your portfolio fluctuate by double-digit percentages in a single day—or even hour—isn't just a test of your financial planning; it's a test of your emotional calibration, narrative resilience, and self-concept. *Volatility doesn't just move markets; it reveals you to yourself.*

This is why volatility tolerance must be treated as a skill, not an innate trait. Like any skill, it can be developed through structured practice, reframing, and intentional exposure. The aim is not to numb yourself or suppress emotion—that's a form of delusion. The goal is to *build internal spaciousness around uncertainty* so that discomfort doesn't automatically trigger reactivity. Emotional agility in volatile environments is not a luxury in this space; it's a competitive edge.

The first foundational insight is this: *volatility is not the same as risk.* Risk refers to the probability of permanent capital loss. Volatility, on the other hand, is price movement—up or down—within a timeframe. Equating the two is a common cognitive error that fuels panic. When prices fall, many interpret it as proof that something is broken, fraudulent, or doomed. But in nascent, speculative markets like crypto, *movement is often driven more by narrative churn, liquidity flows, and emotional contagion than by fundamental collapse.* Understanding this allows you to respond with discernment rather than alarm.

To train for this, one mental model worth integrating is *the volatility window.* Every investment thesis should include a forecast not just of price potential, but of psychological turbulence. Ask yourself: What kind of drawdown would make me question my belief? What kind of sideways stagnation would tempt me to abandon my allocation? If you can't articulate these thresholds clearly, then you haven't sized your position or timed your entry with enough self-awareness. *Practicing volatility begins with anticipating your own breaking points.*

Another essential exercise is *simulated detachment.* Allocate a small, tracked portfolio—real or paper—and commit to checking its balance only once a week, regardless of what happens. During that time, log your emotions separately in a journal. Note the narratives you're telling yourself. Observe when FOMO peaks, when despair sets in, when overconfidence sneaks in after gains. This is not about winning the trade. It's about observing the mental weather system that market exposure activates. *If you cannot observe yourself under stress, you cannot improve your response.*

The role of narrative is paramount here. Most people do not panic because of volatility itself—they panic because they no longer trust their story about what's happening. When your mental model of why an asset has value collapses under pressure, you are left exposed. But if your conviction is grounded in a well-considered thesis—built on research, not memes—then price drops become context, not catastrophes. *The more robust your mental framework, the less fragile your emotional state.*

This is why disciplined re-reading of your original investment rationale during volatility can be clarifying. Ask: Has anything *fundamental* changed? Are the underlying metrics, use case, or roadmap still intact? If so, the volatility is noise. If not, perhaps your thesis needs revisiting. The key is to distinguish between *price action* and *thesis invalidation*—a nuance many fail to parse. One is a reason to pause. The other is a reason to pivot.

There's also value in diversifying the kind of volatility you expose yourself to. This may sound counterintuitive, but expanding your discomfort zone in other domains—physical training, cold exposure, public speaking—can strengthen your general resilience to uncertainty. These are all real-time laboratories for practising response over reaction. The nervous system doesn't differentiate neatly between types of stress. *Becoming someone who can sit with ambiguity in one arena strengthens your ability to do so in others.*

Community plays a role here too, but it must be selected with care. Volatility fuels narrative wars on Twitter, Discord, and Telegram. Groupthink can magnify panic or euphoria with lightning speed. *Surrounding yourself with signal-rich communities—where conviction is grounded in analysis, not emotion—can act as a ballast.* The inverse is also true: If your circle is constantly reacting, it becomes harder to maintain internal steadiness. Choose your informational environment as carefully as you choose your portfolio.

A useful philosophical model to lean on is *stoic volatility*. Derived from ancient Stoic thought, this mindset emphasises the difference between what you can control and what you cannot. You cannot control markets. You cannot control other investors. But you can control your reaction, your posture, your input discipline. Every price movement becomes a kind of dojo—a space to practise returning to internal sovereignty. *The practice is not to control outcomes, but to cultivate equanimity amid flux.*

Reframing is another high-leverage practice. Instead of viewing volatility as something to survive, view it as *tuition.* You are paying in discomfort now to develop wisdom later. Every swing is a lesson in emotional triggers, decision-making under stress, and information filtering. It's not free, but it's formative. *Market experience without pain often produces fragile conviction.* By embracing volatility as the cost of participation in a frontier market, you stop resenting it—and start extracting its teachings.

Some investors use a tactic known as *anchor rebalancing* to stay emotionally grounded. The idea is to define a set of long-term financial or ideological anchors (e.g., "I believe this protocol will be foundational infrastructure for DeFi in five years") and return to them during market swings. These anchors act as emotional checkpoints. If the price deviates but the anchor holds, you stay the course. If the anchor shifts, you adjust. This prevents you from letting temporary fluctuations hijack your deeper time horizon.

It's also critical to distinguish between volatility that signals *health* versus volatility that signals *decay.* In ecosystems with high innovation velocity, user experimentation, and active developer communities, volatility is often a function of organic growth pains. But when volatility is coupled with silence, founder disappearance, or governance disarray, it may reflect fundamental rot. *The presence of volatility isn't always bad. But the context around it matters immensely.*

Finally, recognise the deeper layer of what volatility confronts: our desire for control. Most people enter investing not just to earn returns, but to engineer a sense of mastery over their financial future. Volatility disrupts that illusion. It reminds you that uncertainty is not just a market condition—it's a life condition. Practising volatility, then, is not just financial training. *It's existential training.* It asks you to build a self that can move with instability, not against it. A self that is not fragile in the face of change, because it does not require certainty to function.

The muscle you are building is not stoicism in the flat sense, nor is it naïve optimism. It is *adaptive emotional robustness*—a capacity to stay in contact with your thesis, your risk limits, your principles, and your psychological centre, even when the numbers flash red. That is not only a valuable skill in markets. It is a valuable skill in modern life, where change is constant, narratives shift quickly, and clarity must often be built internally before it can be confirmed externally.

To practise volatility well is to stop trying to predict it—and instead, *train for it.* This means designing systems that honour emotion without being ruled by it. It means building decision processes that anticipate instability, rather than hoping for its absence. And it means turning every downturn into a diagnostic mirror—asking not just "What is the market doing to me?" but "What am I learning about myself from how I'm responding?"

Because in the end, volatility isn't just a price function. It's a psychological teacher. And the students who learn fastest aren't those who avoid it. *They're the ones who build enough internal capacity to sit with it, study it, and keep moving forward regardless.*

Chapter 6
The Wallet Is You – Self-Custody as Identity Formation

What if your most honest résumé wasn't a neatly typeset document at all, but a living archive—an encrypted mosaic of wallet addresses, transaction trails, permissions granted, and on-chain signatures? Imagine if your digital identity, the one that increasingly governs access to capital, collaboration, and credibility, were no longer pinned to a centralised profile but scattered, by design, across a decentralised ledger of intent. This is not speculative fiction. It's already here. In the crypto-native world, the wallet is not simply where you keep your money—it is, in a very real sense, you. And for better or worse, it is fast becoming the primary means by which you are recognised, remembered, and related to.

The word *wallet* feels deceptively quaint—conjuring an image of something that holds coins, cards, perhaps a photograph or two. In the decentralised landscape, however, it is not merely a vessel for assets. It is a locus of agency. Within it, your wealth resides, yes—but so too do your permissions, your verified credentials, the memory of your past engagements. A wallet is less a tool than a medium of selfhood. It's mutable, composable, alive. It reflects not only what you hold, but what you stand for: the projects you've funded, the DAOs where you've cast your vote, the tokens you've quietly refused to offload. In short, it narrates your decisions, not just your balance.

Custody, then, is no longer a purely technical question—it's a philosophical one. As decentralisation redraws the architecture of the web, the way we store and represent ourselves through our wallets becomes an act of personal design, even of existential positioning. Cold storage versus hot wallets is no longer simply convenience versus security—it's a mirror of your relationship with your future self. How much control will you outsource? How much responsibility will you shoulder? To hold your own keys is not merely to reject middlemen; it is to declare that no one will come to save you, and equally, no one will strip you of what's yours.

If you think of it, the parallels to cognition are uncanny. Cold storage is the mind's deep archive: guarded, deliberate, resistant to tampering. A hot wallet is more like working memory: quick, responsive, yet vulnerable. Layering your access resembles the way we tier access to our own recollections—some facts locked away for safekeeping, others instantly retrievable. This is more than a pretty metaphor; it is revealing. The way you manage your crypto often echoes the way you manage your inner order. Disorganised wallets hint at scattered priorities; meticulously indexed holdings betray an underlying discipline. In this light, storage becomes a form of self-regulation.

But wallets aren't only about self-reflection—they are swiftly becoming passports in a widening digital polity. An ENS domain or other alias can serve as your public-facing pseudonym. Your transaction history becomes proof of your credibility. Your record of joining launches, minting NFTs, or voting on governance proposals shapes how others read your integrity, your cultural alignment. In a disintermediated web, your on-chain actions are your résumé—your reputational collateral. Whether you're applying for a DAO role, signalling allegiance to a movement, or courting investors, the wallet speaks, loudly.

Here, personal branding shifts. It is no longer about the polish of what you *say*, but the undeniability of what you *sign*. On-chain proof replaces the flattering gloss of the traditional CV. You cannot embellish a ledger entry; it states plainly that you held, staked, funded, or declined. Such radical transparency is double-edged: it grants trust, yet exposes patterns. It demands a new vigilance—one that asks whether to compartmentalise activities across wallets, obscure certain actions, or cultivate your digital self with the same deliberation you bring to your public life offline.

None of this is theory. In a world where transactions endure indefinitely, each carries reputational mass. Back every passing meme coin, and that exuberance is recorded. Defraud others, and the stain is permanent. Champion high-integrity ventures, and that commitment shines through. Unlike deletable centralised profiles, a wallet is a living chronicle—prompting a form of self-awareness that is behavioural rather than declarative.

Yet here lies a tension. We are promised privacy and sovereignty, yet the ledger engraves our choices for all to see. We operate under pseudonyms, yet these aliases congeal into enduring identities. We embrace decentralisation, yet gravitate to dominant wallet tools and naming systems that risk becoming centralised choke points in all but name. The challenge is to shape a digital self that honours autonomy while retaining coherence. That is the real frontier—not only where you place your assets, but how you construct your presence.

One emerging tactic is intentional wallet separation. Much like maintaining separate email accounts for work, personal life, and passions, crypto users are now dividing their activities: speculative trading in one wallet, governance work in another, long-term holdings in a third. This isn't just neat housekeeping—it's emotional insulation. A trading loss in one arena needn't taint your sense of stewardship in another. Boundaries support clarity; clarity underpins sovereignty.

Still, no structure can stand without philosophical foundation. The deeper question is not "Where do I keep my tokens?" but "What sort of person am I becoming through my engagement with these assets?" Are you shaping the ecosystem, or merely orbiting it? Playing a short-term game, or building a long-term edifice? Do you outsource trust, or bear it yourself? These are questions of character disguised as questions of security—and the wallet, increasingly, is where they are answered.

This chapter will not drown you in cold-storage manuals or security audits, though those have their place. Instead, it will trace the links between custody decisions and the values they silently encode—between the design of your digital containers and the narrative you wish them to tell. We will consider how wallets forge reputations, orchestrate communities, and scaffold the selves we are in the process of becoming.

Because self-custody, in the end, is not simply an operational choice. It is a statement of identity. And the way you weave that choice into the fabric of your digital life will determine not just what you own—but who you are when the ledger looks back.

Not Your Keys, Not Your Self:

The phrase "Not your keys, not your coins" has long been a rallying cry among crypto purists—an unambiguous warning against custodial complacency. But beneath its surface-level technicality lies a deeper truth, one that transcends asset ownership and enters the terrain of personal sovereignty: *not your keys, not your self.* This isn't just about who holds your tokens. It's about who defines your identity, who controls your agency, and who determines the parameters of your participation in the digital age. The act of self-custody—of taking full responsibility for one's assets—becomes not just a security protocol, but a philosophical position. To hold your own keys is to claim authorship over your digital existence.

Autonomy in the decentralised world begins with the question of control, but it doesn't end there. Control is the initial layer—the keypair in your possession, the seed phrase memorised or stored. But layered atop control is *consequence.* When you alone can move funds, sign transactions, or verify identity, there is no safety net, no password reset, no customer support. There is only you—and the systems you choose to trust or not trust. In this way, self-custody serves as a crucible. It demands that you reconcile your appetite for freedom with your tolerance for responsibility. It reveals whether you are prepared to own the outcomes of your digital actions—not just the profitable ones.

This has far-reaching implications for identity formation. In a world where social media platforms, financial institutions, and governments serve as the default identity arbiters, the decentralised model introduces a radical alternative: *self-sovereign identity.* Here, you are not a user granted conditional access. You are a node with inherent permission. Your wallet doesn't ask who you are—it *proves* who you are through cryptographic integrity and transactional history. This flips the logic of access. In the traditional model, identity precedes activity—you must *be someone* before you are allowed to *do something.* In crypto, activity *is* identity. What you sign, stake, and support becomes your credential. You are what you verify.

This inversion, while empowering, is also disorienting. Most people are not trained to define themselves outside of external validation structures. From school grades to job titles, from citizenship documents to social media bios, identity has long been scaffolded by institutional approval. To replace those structures with decentralised proofs—non-transferable tokens, signed attestations, on-chain behaviour—requires a redefinition not just of credentials, but of self-concept. It raises uncomfortable questions: *Who am I if no one vouches for me? What is status in a system where status cannot be faked? What does it mean to be seen, when visibility is a function of transparency, not performance?*

These are not merely technological dilemmas. They are existential. They push us to examine what we actually mean by "ownership" in a world where digital assets are borderless, programmable, and permanent. When you self-custody a token, you're not just storing value—you're declaring intent. You're choosing to participate in an ecosystem on your terms. You're declining the safety and convenience of intermediaries in favour of the discomfort of full accountability. And in doing so, you are shaping a version of yourself that is harder to manipulate, harder to cancel, and harder to forget. *To own your keys is to own your consequences.*

Yet this isn't a binary proposition. There is no singular, correct way to approach self-custody. Some use hardware wallets with multi-signature backups. Others split keys across trusted parties. Some rely on social recovery, while others opt for seed phrase vaults. The point is not ideological purity. The point is *conscious design.* Sovereignty is not a default state—it's a configuration, one that must be revisited and recalibrated as the context changes. What matters is not that you hold your keys, but that you *understand why you do—or why you don't.* Passive dependence on platforms is not inherently wrong. But *unexamined dependence always is.*

The psychological shift required for true digital autonomy is substantial. Most people have been conditioned to outsource trust: to banks for their money, to companies for their data, to governments for their identity. Reclaiming that trust—and internalising its risks—demands a new kind of emotional infrastructure. It requires resilience against fear, clarity amidst uncertainty, and discipline without oversight. These are not technical skills. They are character traits. And they do not emerge from tutorials or user guides. They emerge from *practice.* Each time you manage a transaction without assistance, you reinforce your agency. Each time you recover from a mistake without blame, you reinforce your adaptability. Over time, these micro-acts of autonomy become the foundation of a new digital self—not fragile, but *anti-fragile.*

This shift has profound implications for how we understand community as well. Traditional communities are often bound by shared geography, ideology, or ethnicity. In decentralised ecosystems, communities are bound by *shared responsibility.* A DAO is not just a club—it is a governance body where every member bears the cost of apathy. A validator set is not just infrastructure—it is a social contract among those who choose to shoulder the burden of uptime and honesty. In these spaces, there is no institutional babysitter. There is only the collective will to coordinate. *Self-custody becomes the atomic unit of trust.* Without it, the organism fails.

Of course, this introduces tension. Not everyone wants to be their own bank. Not everyone wants the burden of sovereignty. The illusion of freedom can quickly become a prison of responsibility if the user lacks preparation or support. This is why educational efforts around custody must go beyond how-to guides. They must speak to *readiness.* They must articulate the psychological, philosophical, and practical demands of digital autonomy. Too often, the community conflates technical literacy with preparedness. But one can know how to use a hardware wallet and still be emotionally unready to bear its weight.

This is also where the limits of decentralisation become most visible. Total independence can lead to isolation. And trustlessness, when taken too far, becomes paranoia. The ideal is not radical individualism. It is *intentional interdependence*—a network of sovereign individuals who choose to coordinate, not because they are forced to, but because they see value in doing so. The goal is not to be alone. The goal is to be *uncoerced.* And the infrastructure of self-custody is what makes that possible.

Philosophically, we are entering a phase where key management is no longer just a security concern—it's a narrative concern. Your keys are the axis around which your digital story spins. Lose them, and you lose not just access, but continuity. No other technology so clearly ties technical action to existential continuity. In that sense, self-custody is a form of *memory work*. It's about preserving identity across time. It's about remaining legible to yourself across changing protocols, platforms, and paradigms. It's about designing a self that is not just reactive, but sovereign—one who acts with clarity, because they are governed from within, not managed from without.

This chapter explores these themes with rigour and depth. We will not evangelise self-custody blindly, nor dismiss its complexities. Instead, we will explore it as a layered practice—part operational, part philosophical, entirely consequential. We will interrogate the cultural narratives that shape our views on responsibility, the technical tools that enable autonomy, and the human tendencies that make sovereignty both empowering and daunting. And we will argue that *to hold your keys is not just to own your assets—it is to own your authorship*. Your story. Your stakes. Your future.

Because if you don't hold the keys to your own life—someone else will.

Cold Storage, Warm Mind:

The modern mind is under siege—not just from the chaos of markets or the deluge of data, but from the absence of durable systems to hold what truly matters. This isn't merely a digital problem; it's a psychological one. In the world of crypto, where value is both intangible and irreversible, the concept of *storage* carries weight far beyond private keys and seed phrases. How we choose to hold our assets mirrors how we choose to hold our thoughts, memories, and identity. Cold storage isn't just a best practice in asset protection—it's a metaphor for how we manage risk, scarcity, and permanence in an increasingly fluid world. *To store well is to think well.*

At its most basic level, crypto storage divides into two broad categories: hot wallets and cold wallets. Hot wallets—whether browser extensions, mobile apps, or exchange-based custodial options—are connected to the internet and offer convenience at the cost of vulnerability. Cold wallets—such as hardware devices, air-gapped computers, or even paper keys—remove that network exposure entirely, storing private keys offline. The security trade-off is immediate: hot wallets are like keeping cash in your pocket—fast, accessible, but always at risk. Cold wallets are like vaults—slow, deliberate, but resistant to intrusion.

But beneath these technical distinctions lies something more instructive: a philosophy of intentionality. Cold storage is not about paranoia—it's about selectivity. It forces a pause, a decision point, a moment of reflection. You don't casually transact from cold storage. You plan. You assess. You prioritise. This mirrors the cognitive distinction between working memory and long-term memory. Just as we don't keep every idea at the surface of consciousness, we don't keep every asset exposed to the livewire of the internet. *We tuck away what matters—not to forget it, but to protect it until it matters again.*

The act of moving funds to cold storage is a statement of belief: that some assets are not for speculation, not for impulse, but for preservation. It mirrors the mindset of legacy—what do I want to last beyond noise, hype, and distraction? What do I value enough to make inconvenient, so it can remain uncorrupted? In this sense, cold storage becomes a ritual of clarity. It separates signal from noise. The investor who uses cold storage well is the same kind of person who journals deliberately, curates their commitments, or deletes apps to regain cognitive bandwidth. *The discipline of decentralised finance is, at heart, a discipline of self.*

There's also an architectural lesson embedded in crypto storage strategies—one that speaks directly to how we organise information, identity, and intent. Consider the tiered storage systems that many experienced users adopt: a small hot wallet for daily interaction, a secondary wallet for mid-term exposure, and a hardware wallet or multisig vault for high-value holdings. This isn't just financial hygiene—it's modularity in action. It reflects a layered cognition: what must be immediately available, what can sit in mid-term recall, and what should remain foundational but rarely accessed. The mind, too, thrives when structured this way. *We don't need everything all the time—we need what matters, when it matters, in the right context.*

Self-custody demands a clarity of intention that most financial systems have abstracted away. There is no 'forgot password' in a cold wallet. No helpline to retrieve your seed phrase. Every protocol, every step, is a mirror to your mindfulness. This is confronting, but it's also liberating. There is dignity in being fully responsible—if, and only if, you are prepared for the weight that comes with it. Much like mindfulness practice, self-custody is not about control alone. It's about awareness. *Every moment you interact with your storage setup is an opportunity to ask: am I acting with clarity, or just reacting with convenience?*

The tension between convenience and control is not new, but crypto makes it visible in ways traditional finance never could. Banks abstract risk. Apps abstract identity. Cloud services abstract memory. But in crypto, the architecture is naked. You see the seed phrase. You sign the transaction. You verify the address. This exposure can be disorienting at first, but it also recalibrates your relationship to responsibility. In the same way that writing longhand forces you to think differently than typing, using cold storage forces you to relate differently to your assets. It slows you down—*and in a culture addicted to speed, slowness is revolutionary.*

There are also emotional dimensions to crypto storage that are often overlooked. Cold storage can offer peace of mind—but only if you've done the uncomfortable work of setting it up properly. If not, it becomes a locus of anxiety: Where did I put the seed phrase? Did I verify the firmware? What if I die—who can access it? These are not minor questions. They are the same questions we ask about wills, medical directives, and family photos. What survives when I don't? What gets passed on, and what gets lost forever? Cold storage, when approached with intentionality, becomes part of a *legacy stack*. It is not just where we store our wealth—it is how we encode meaning across time.

This brings us to the core analogy of this chapter: storage as mind. Think of your mental landscape as a kind of portfolio—populated with thoughts, memories, fears, and principles. Most people's mental lives are cluttered, impulsive, and scattered. Everything is hot. Everything is live. There is no archive, no cold tier where deep convictions or long-term goals can rest undisturbed. The consequence is mental volatility—overreaction, regret, confusion. But what if we treated our minds like we treat our wallets? What if we created layers, compartments, safeguards? *What if we were as careful with our thoughts as we are with our tokens?*

Mental cold storage is the act of consciously shelving ideas, values, and plans that matter deeply—but don't need constant access. It's the difference between reacting to every news cycle and having a long-term philosophy. It's the difference between tracking every price swing and having conviction in your thesis. When we mimic this architecture in our interior lives, we become more stable, more focused, and more resilient. We gain the ability to *pause before panic.* To *choose response over reaction.* To *store, not suppress.* In a world of algorithmic triggers and social volatility, this is a kind of superpower.

Of course, cold storage is not without risk. Devices fail. Backups get lost. Human error creeps in. But this, too, mirrors life. Even our best systems are imperfect. What matters is redundancy, review, and recovery. Just as you test your wallet restoration process, you must test your mental assumptions. Just as you split your key among trusted parties, you must split your truths across mentors, peers, and reflections. Storage is not a one-time act. It is a living, revisitable process. *It demands maintenance, not just setup.*

The final insight here is cultural. As digital natives increasingly build lives that are wallet-first rather than nation-first or bank-first, the metaphor of storage will expand. A person's cold wallet will not just be a vault—it will be a time capsule, an archive of values, a memory bank. Transactions will be not just transfers, but traces—articulating what they cared about, supported, and believed. This shifts storage from a technical necessity to a narrative tool. Your wallet is not just what you hold. *It's who you were when you decided to hold it.* And cold storage, in that sense, becomes a kind of memory palace—less volatile, more enduring, and deeply human.

To store well, in crypto and in life, is to care enough about something to protect it from noise, haste, and compromise. It is an act of reverence, a strategy of resilience, and a philosophy of design. Cold storage is not cold-hearted. It is not detachment. It is not avoidance. It is a sign that you've thought about what matters—and that you've built a structure to honour it. A warm mind is not one that touches everything all the time. It is one that knows when to hold, when to let go, and when to step back—because *what you protect reveals what you value.* And what you value reveals who you are becoming.

"Identity in the Age of Wallets"

A wallet used to be a place to store money. Now, increasingly, it's a window into who you are. In decentralised ecosystems, your wallet address is not merely a tool for financial transactions—it is a public ledger of behaviour, taste, allegiance, and values. It's becoming a résumé you don't write but one you live. And unlike a traditional CV, it cannot be polished or faked. It is immutable, timestamped, and verified. What you own, where you've participated, what you've supported—all of it is etched into a digital trail that will outlive most social media platforms and institutional records. *Identity is no longer declared. It's inferred—on-chain.*

Consider the difference between claiming to care about environmental causes and actually staking into a climate-related DAO, purchasing carbon offset NFTs, or contributing to green protocols. The former is a statement; the latter is a record. It becomes provable, traceable, and context-rich. In this sense, your crypto wallet is more than a financial instrument. It is a form of biographical truth. What used to be optional is becoming inevitable. As more economic, social, and civic functions migrate to blockchains, *the wallet becomes the new ID*—except this ID is active, evolving, and shaped by voluntary participation rather than bureaucratic issuance.

This shift has implications that extend far beyond the confines of crypto culture. Web3-native hiring practices are already emerging where employers examine wallet activity to assess fit: Does this candidate actually engage with governance? Have they contributed to key protocols? Are they early adopters or passive holders? Unlike LinkedIn endorsements, wallet data resists inflation. You either voted in the proposal or you didn't. You deployed capital into risky projects before they were mainstream or you followed the crowd later. *Your credibility isn't self-proclaimed. It's cryptographically encoded.*

But it isn't just about proving competence. Wallets are also emerging as social and cultural filters. Membership in NFT communities, DAO treasuries, or protocol contributor pools subtly signal affinities and aesthetic values. A wallet heavy in meme coins suggests a different persona than one focused on decentralised infrastructure or privacy tools. And yet both can be valid identities. This is precisely the point: *the wallet is not a uniform—it's a mosaic.* Unlike traditional social profiles, which flatten identity into curated images and status updates, wallets are multidimensional. They show activity, intention, risk appetite, and ideological bent—all without saying a word.

This evolution puts pressure on old categories. Where once reputation was built through institutions—your alma mater, your employer, your title—it is now increasingly composable. In the decentralised world, your credentials are fragmented across protocols, timelines, and tokens. But they can be recombined and read. A DeFi yield farmer, a GitHub contributor, and a DAO moderator may all occupy the same wallet address, forming a composite identity that is more nuanced than any job title could capture. *Web3 doesn't eliminate identity—it multiplies it, then lets others interpret.*

There is, of course, a trade-off. The transparency that gives wallet-based identity its credibility also exposes users to new vulnerabilities. If your entire financial and participatory history is public, privacy becomes a scarce resource. This opens up ethical questions: Should employers be evaluating people based on their on-chain history? What counts as signal versus noise? Are early trades permanent stains or early signs of experimentation? In a world where your first NFT mint or poorly timed investment is permanently etched on-chain, *does forgiveness exist?*

Some have tried to solve this with secondary or "burner" wallets—compartmentalised identities for different functions. But even these can be tracked and correlated through transaction patterns and IP data. Others lean into pseudonymity, letting wallet addresses or ENS handles act as masks behind which identity can be fluid. Yet even here, behavioural consistency builds narrative. Over time, every address accrues a kind of reputation, whether intended or not. *In crypto, you're always leaving a trail—even when you're trying to disappear.*

The social implications are complex. In some ways, wallet-based identity flattens privilege. It doesn't care where you were born or what university you attended. It cares what you've done, what you've risked, and what you've supported. In other ways, it introduces new forms of bias. Wealthy wallets carry more influence in governance. Rare NFT holders gain access to private groups. Those early to certain tokens can afford to be louder than those who arrived later. *Status re-emerges, but in different clothing.* The mechanisms may be decentralised, but the outcomes still require scrutiny.

There's also a new psychology at play. Knowing that every action is recorded, visible, and durable may induce paralysis—or hyper-curation. Users begin to second-guess their transactions not just for cost or strategy, but for reputational optics. Should I buy this NFT? Not just because I like it, but because it will appear in my wallet. Should I sell this token? Not just for profit, but because it might suggest I'm abandoning a community. The result is a new kind of self-awareness—one that blends financial literacy with social signalling. *Every transaction becomes a micro-performance of identity.*

Yet this also opens the door to intentionality. If wallets are going to be read as résumés, then we should treat them as such. This doesn't mean becoming performative. It means becoming *conscious.* Designing your wallet's contents becomes an act of personal strategy. What projects do you want to be affiliated with? What risks are you willing to take in public? Which communities do you want to signal allegiance to? It's not just what you invest in—it's what you endorse. And in a decentralised world where allegiance is fluid, those choices matter more than ever.

One particularly interesting development is the emergence of wallet-based reputation tools—protocols that score or rank addresses based on past behaviour. These systems aim to formalise trust in environments where identity is fluid and often pseudonymous. For example, on-chain credit scoring models assess repayment history for decentralised loans, while reputation layers for DAOs weight voting power by contribution rather than token count. These tools aren't perfect, but they signal a move towards richer, more interpretable forms of identity. *A wallet is no longer a void—it's a vocabulary.*

Looking ahead, wallets may become the central organising structure of digital identity—not just in crypto, but in the broader digital economy. Already, we see this in the growing use of wallets for sign-ins, credential verifications, and access permissions. Instead of creating usernames and passwords, users connect a wallet. Instead of submitting a PDF résumé, they share a wallet snapshot. Instead of trusting institutions, platforms trust cryptographic proof. This is a radical shift—one that moves identity from assertion to verification, from reputation by proxy to reputation by pattern.

But we must be cautious. Wallet-based identity has the potential to either empower or entrench. If used thoughtfully, it decentralises power, lowers barriers, and amplifies underrepresented voices. If used recklessly, it could become yet another mechanism of exclusion—opaque, gamed, and unequally distributed. The challenge lies not in the technology, but in the governance surrounding it. How we interpret, weight, and contextualise wallet data will determine whether this new form of identity is liberating or limiting. *Tools don't create justice. People do.*

Ultimately, to understand your wallet is to understand your trajectory—not just financially, but philosophically. It shows your risk tolerance, your ideological leanings, your priorities. It is a public, living document of belief. And unlike a social media feed, it's not just about what you say. It's about what you do. The wallet is action over aesthetics. Commitment over commentary. And in that sense, it is *far more honest than most self-presentations we see today.*

So the next time you open your wallet app, don't just check your balance. Ask yourself what story it tells. What future it points toward. And whether the choices it reveals are aligned with the self you're trying to become. Because in this age, your wallet isn't just what you have. *It's who you are becoming.*

"Designing Your Digital Self"

The modern self is no longer confined to flesh and passport. It's distributed—across blockchains, across wallets, across networks. In a decentralised world, identity is not granted by institutions; it is composed, iterated, and broadcast through one's actions, holdings, affiliations, and public keys. The question is no longer whether you have a digital identity. You already do. The question is whether it was designed or defaulted—whether it reflects intention or inertia. *To design your digital self is to take authorship over the only identity that is both portable and permanent.*

In traditional systems, identity was passive. You were issued documentation, categorised by demographic fields, and assessed through institutional records. In the decentralised world, you build reputation not through claims but through cryptographic evidence. Every on-chain interaction—every token you hold, every DAO you join, every NFT you mint—is a brushstroke on the canvas of your digital personhood. It's not simply what you say you believe. It's what you *do* that gets recorded, verified, and displayed. This changes everything. *You are what you commit to.*

This shift toward composable identity is more than a technical curiosity—it is a philosophical reorientation. It introduces autonomy with accountability. You're no longer relying on third parties to define or validate you. Instead, you construct your digital presence one transaction, one credential, one wallet at a time. But like any powerful tool, this freedom demands structure. Without design, your digital self risks becoming a patchwork of impulse—an unedited stream of exposures and associations that may not align with your goals, beliefs, or values. *Intentional design is not aesthetic. It is existential.*

Begin by asking: What should your presence *say* about you? Not to impress, but to express. Are you signalling curiosity or conviction? Experimentation or mastery? What kinds of communities do you support? Which protocols do you trust? Are you building, investing, governing—or observing? Every one of these decisions leaves a trace. In aggregate, they form a reputational architecture others will read, interpret, and respond to. Whether you opt for a pseudonymous handle or full doxxed transparency, *your actions will become your signal.*

Consider the case of ENS (Ethereum Name Service). Assigning a human-readable name to your address is not just a convenience—it's a form of claiming space, of anchoring your identity in a sea of keys and hashes. Similarly, linking your wallet to a public social profile, or using it to vote in governance proposals, elevates it from a passive container to an active agent. These are small acts with outsized impact. *They demonstrate that digital identity is not just about storage—it's about stance.*

This idea is particularly visible in the NFT space. Here, ownership becomes biography. The collections in your wallet can suggest your taste, your humour, your values. But unlike Instagram feeds, which are endlessly editable, NFTs are durable. Selling one or buying another has consequence. Over time, your wallet becomes a gallery others visit—not to observe your wealth, but to infer your worldview. This is why some users maintain separate wallets for experimentation versus long-term holdings: *not all selves are ready for the same level of exposure.*

Designing your digital self also requires an awareness of context. In Web3, identities are fluid across platforms—but they're also legible. What you do in one protocol informs how you're perceived in another. A respected contributor in one DAO can earn instant credibility elsewhere. A reckless trader or spammy airdrop hunter might find themselves informally blacklisted by peers. Unlike Web2, where identity is siloed by app, Web3 surfaces coherence. *Your presence must hold up across environments.*

This coherence doesn't mean uniformity. In fact, one of the most powerful aspects of decentralised identity is its modularity. You can maintain multiple wallets for distinct purposes—professional, experimental, philanthropic, pseudonymous. Each becomes a facet of a larger truth. But even this requires conscious curation. What connects them? How will you cross-reference or separate them? Which one do you link to a proposal? Which one do you sign with? Designing your digital self is not about creating one identity—it's about *orchestrating identities with integrity.*

Future-proofing your identity also means thinking beyond trend cycles. A meme token may offer quick clout, but what does it add to your long-term arc? A speculative NFT flip might generate gains, but does it align with your narrative of value? These aren't moral questions. They're design ones. They ask whether your behaviour is building towards a vision—or simply reacting to noise. The most respected participants in decentralised systems are not always the loudest or richest. They are the most *legible*, the most *reliable*, the most *aligned.*

Alignment, in this context, means consistency between intention and action. Do your transactions reflect your stated values? Do your governance votes match your public positions? Does your participation in communities go deeper than optics? When people view your on-chain history, are they encountering coherence or contradiction? These aren't aesthetic concerns—they're functional ones. They determine trust, influence, and opportunity. *Digital identity is no longer a presentation. It's a protocol.*

This brings us to the emotional aspect of design. Unlike curated social media profiles, a digital identity in Web3 is often exposed to scrutiny, misunderstanding, and permanence. Transactions can't be deleted. Early missteps can be traced. Reputations, once lost, are difficult to rebuild. This adds pressure—but also invites maturity. It rewards those who are willing to think long-term, act transparently, and navigate complexity with humility. *Your digital self must be durable—not just visible.*

One forward-thinking approach is to treat your wallet not as a container, but as a curriculum vitae in motion. Ask yourself periodically: What does this wallet say about my evolution? Am I growing? Diversifying? Deepening my expertise? Which protocols have I contributed to meaningfully, not just passively? What causes have I materially supported? Which experiments failed, and which matured? Reflecting on your digital self with the same care you might devote to a career path or artistic portfolio shifts the frame from consumption to composition. *You are not just participating in Web3. You are publishing your identity through it.*

It's also worth remembering that wallet-based identity is still young. Standards are evolving. New forms of on-chain credentials—such as Soulbound tokens, verifiable credentials, and ZK reputation scores—are emerging. These tools offer richer ways to prove skill, contribution, and trustworthiness without sacrificing privacy. Designing your digital self means staying literate in these tools, but not being seduced by every new feature. The goal is not maximal exposure, but *intentional coherence.*

At a cultural level, this evolution marks a return to craftsmanship. Just as artisans once signed their work, crypto-native identities are signed with action. A clean, purposeful wallet is the new calling card. It invites collaboration. It earns access. It shapes perception. Not through branding campaigns or follower counts, but through verifiable, decentralised history. In this sense, *reputation in Web3 is not spoken—it is staked.*

Ultimately, designing your digital self is not about performance. It's about presence. It's about making visible what you stand for, what you build, and what you're willing to be held accountable to. In a decentralised world, the self is not fixed, but *forkable*—it evolves through choices, affiliations, and contributions. The only constant is the design: deliberate or not. Thoughtful or not. Clear or cluttered. And just like any system, the quality of the output depends on the clarity of the architecture.

So before your next transaction, before your next protocol interaction or NFT mint, pause. Ask: What is this action adding to my digital self? Does it reflect the future I want to be part of? Is it noise, or is it signal? Because long after the market has moved on, long after headlines fade, your actions will remain—etched on-chain, open to interpretation, impossible to delete. And over time, they will speak louder than anything you could ever say. *Your digital identity is your design—own it before someone else defines it for you.*

Chapter 7
The Long Game – Thinking Generationally in a Hype-Driven Market

In crypto, the rarest skill is not coding brilliance, secure custody, or even shrewd capital deployment—it is patience. In a culture addicted to urgency, where 10x headlines flood every feed and overnight fortunes are spun into morality tales disguised as inspiration, the act of holding steady—of thinking in decades rather than days—feels almost subversive. Yet the deepest transformations promised by decentralised technologies will not reveal themselves in quarterly charts. They will emerge slowly, over decades. And the investor who can think in terms of legacy will reap returns not only in wealth, but in perspective.

At its heart, crypto is infrastructure. But unlike the roads or railways that reshaped past centuries, its blueprints are largely invisible. They reside in wallets, private keys, protocols, and conviction. Much like the internet's earliest champions—those who endured public scepticism, false starts, and endless regulatory headwinds before it became the backbone of modern life—crypto believers must see past the noise to the long arc of its potential. Volatility is the price of entry. Attention is the stake. And the reward, if you can hold your ground while others lose theirs, is generational optionality.

Recasting crypto as legacy rather than lottery is not a refusal to face risk; it is a recalibration of the lens. The lottery mindset chases peaks, times exits, celebrates sudden spikes, and broods over missed moons. The legacy mindset, by contrast, assesses assets the way one might assess farmland or a centuries-old trust: Will this matter in thirty years? Is it foundational or fleeting? Does it build resilience or hollow it out?

When Satoshi released the Bitcoin whitepaper in 2008, there was no promise of riches—only a proposal for a new system of trust. What followed was not merely a market, but a movement—a gradual, global reconsideration of money, governance, and ownership in the digital sphere. That it now trades ceaselessly in open markets does not dilute its seriousness; it heightens the responsibility of those who hold it. Every time crypto is treated as a fleeting punt rather than a long-term trust, its potential shrinks. Every time we resist that impulse, we help it endure as time-resistant capital.

Decentralised wealth carries a peculiar irony: the greater the control it grants, the greater the demands it places on its holder. There is no helpline for lost keys. No central bank to undo a rash decision. And yet this independence makes possible a new type of family inheritance—one in which values, access, and education can be encoded alongside the assets themselves. Estate planning in this world moves beyond lawyers and wills; it becomes a matter of seed phrases, hardware devices, and generational fluency.

This emerging craft—crypto estate architecture—is not purely technical. It is moral. How do you grant access across generations without suffocating autonomy? How do you ensure heirs inherit not only wealth, but the judgement to wield it wisely? These are not side issues; they are the core design challenge. In crypto, a single misstep—misplaced keys, unclear instructions—can erase a legacy entirely. Self-custody may be the purest act of trust. But legacy demands translation.

That translation is as much about mindset as it is about money. The cultural inheritance of crypto—its ethos, its cautionary tales, its governance models—may outlast the coins themselves. Teaching a child to parse an Ethereum transaction, to spot a rug pull, to cast a DAO vote—these are modern forms of empowerment. Tomorrow's digital wallets will be more than vaults. They will be archives of contribution.

Holding a long view in a market built for short-term dopamine is not easy. Platforms reward constant movement. Charts tempt emotional reaction. Social media celebrates commentary over contemplation. Yet the most successful crypto holders of the past decade were rarely the ones constantly in motion. They were the ones who stepped back. Who thought like architects rather than gamblers. Who treated their assets as orchards to be cultivated, not slot machines to be yanked. Long-term investing in crypto is not idleness; it is purposeful restraint. It is the quiet work of building systems—cold storage, steady contributions, delegated voting rights—that allow you to do less, not more.

This stands in sharp contrast to the norms of traditional finance, where skill is equated with swift reaction. There, the ideal investor anticipates, reallocates, and responds in rapid cycles. Crypto exposes the flaw in this reflex. The decentralised future will favour not the fastest, but the best prepared. Not those scrambling for the next airdrop, but those patiently building durable presence. And building is slow work. It asks for calm and a deliberate detachment from hype.

There is still room for experimentation—measured exploration of new protocols, early-stage projects, or evolving ecosystems. But for the long-term thinker, such risk-taking is layered, not lurching. It sits apart from the core. It is documented. It is taught. It is reviewed yearly, not hourly. Its success is measured not in spikes, but in clarity.

Resisting the crypto culture of "status-through-speed" is itself an act of defiance. Here, slowness is often confused with ignorance. Reflection with irrelevance. And yet, history reminds us: enduring fortunes are rarely made in public, and never in haste. The wisest capital in this space is already shifting focus—from exit surges to sovereign portfolios, from coin hype to custody discipline, from speculation to succession.

This final point is not optional. Crypto has entered the human inheritance stream. What began as a fringe financial experiment now stands as an estate asset, a family trust, a bearer of both identity and ideology. That reality imposes a duty on early adopters—not simply to accumulate, but to prepare. The relevant question has moved beyond "Should I own crypto?" to "Am I building something that can outlive me?"

This requires a broader redefinition of wealth. Crypto, when seen through the lens of legacy, is not about speed of gain but depth of design. Time horizons clarify purpose. Conversations about digital assets can forge unexpected family intimacy. And systems—technical, emotional, philosophical—can be shaped to honour the present while guarding the future. What began as a technological experiment is now a crucible for legacy. Not what you can flip, but what you can leave.

The long game is demanding. It asks for restraint in a culture wired for reaction. Foresight in a space that prizes immediacy. But for those willing to widen the frame—to think in generations, not months—it offers something precious: the chance to build wealth that grows, adapts, and persists. Wealth that is more than capital; wealth as continuity.

Our task, then, is not to win the day. It is to shape the years ahead—and to ensure that when we hand over the keys, we hand over understanding. What we build now should not be aimed at tomorrow's price chart, but tomorrow's custodians. The true legacy of crypto lies not in sovereignty alone, but in stewardship. Not merely in freedom, but in foresight. And for those prepared to play the long game, the rewards will not be measured solely in profit. They will be measured in permanence.

Wealth vs Riches:

The crypto markets have created millionaires overnight and erased fortunes just as quickly. It's a domain where volatility is often mistaken for velocity, and where surface-level success is flaunted as wisdom. But beneath the adrenaline-fuelled exchanges, speculative manias, and NFT-driven headlines lies a more subtle, foundational inquiry—one that matters far more than portfolio snapshots: *Do you want to be rich, or do you want to be wealthy?*

The distinction is not semantic. It is structural. *Riches are numerical; wealth is behavioural.* Riches can be counted; wealth must be carried. Riches might impress on social media or fund a luxurious weekend; wealth builds options, resilience, and time. One is event-driven. The other is identity-rooted. *Riches arrive fast and exit faster. Wealth stays.* It is a relationship not with money, but with meaning.

This may seem like a rhetorical flourish, but it has very real-world implications. The person who wins a crypto lottery—buying a memecoin before it spikes, flipping an NFT at the right time—is not necessarily any closer to being free than they were the day before. In fact, sudden riches often entrap rather than emancipate. They attract attention without offering tools. They create noise without wisdom. Riches do not inherently lead to clarity. *More money in the absence of deeper thinking merely scales chaos.*

By contrast, wealth is cumulative and intentional. It is built, not won. It is grounded in habits, systems, and frameworks—many of which run counter to the culture of constant trading and algorithmic adrenaline. Wealth respects context. It acknowledges taxes, inflation, burn rate, liquidity, key management, and long-term viability. It understands volatility not as threat or thrill, but as terrain. *It builds the muscles to walk across it soberly.*

Wealth also implies sovereignty. Riches, especially in the crypto context, are often dependent on external validation: the right token mooning, the right influencer reposting, the right trend catching fire. But those signals are inherently unstable. Wealth doesn't chase. It sets structure. It is less concerned with the day's candle and more focused on asset durability, strategic exposure, and the architecture of custody. *Wealth makes you independent of noise. Riches amplify your dependence on it.*

This is especially critical in a space as novel and decentralised as crypto, where narratives shift rapidly and price can be divorced from fundamentals. It's easy to confuse luck with competence. A single trade can inflate a sense of genius that reality does not confirm. In such environments, psychological calibration becomes the differentiator. Those who understand the difference between riches and wealth tend to exit the screen and enter the spreadsheet. *They ask not "How much did I make?" but "How much does this help me not need to chase the next?"*

Let's consider what wealth *actually* looks like in practice: it's a diversified, risk-adjusted portfolio with long-term custody solutions. It includes frameworks for estate planning, even if modest. It may include off-chain assets, legal wrappers, clear operating principles, and conscious spending habits. It's informed by education, not entertainment. It's underpinned by time preference and emotional control. *It is measured not just by what's owned, but by what's understood.*

None of this means there is no place for fast gains. Speculation, when done with guardrails, can be a valid strategy. There is value in momentum plays, asymmetric bets, and early-stage conviction. But the point is that speculation must sit *inside* a system—not *replace* it. It must be calibrated, not compulsive. It should enhance wealth, not distract from it. And more often than not, the most durable gains are not those chased under pressure, but those held through discipline.

This is where ambition requires recalibration. Many people enter crypto with dreams of escape velocity—of quitting jobs, buying islands, disappearing from responsibility. But true wealth, paradoxically, is less about escape and more about stewardship. It's about *constructing* a life that is coherent, flexible, and sustainable—not just financially, but psychologically. Being rich might buy you an exit; being wealthy gives you optionality. It buys back your *attention.*

Another difference: *Riches are singular; wealth is shared.* The pursuit of riches often fosters secrecy, competition, and individualism. Wealth, by contrast, enables community—whether through education, generosity, or design. When you're wealthy in knowledge, in time, and in orientation, you are better positioned to mentor, teach, and uplift. You become a node of clarity in an ecosystem often clouded by hype. *You become a stabiliser, not a speculator.*

This matters more than ever in a world where digital assets are redefining social contracts. Wallets are becoming identity layers. DAOs are emerging as vehicles for group ownership. Communities are forming around shared purpose rather than proximity. In this setting, what you *represent* matters as much as what you *hold.* Wealth radiates competence, reliability, and depth. Riches simply announce price.

Let's take a real-world example: imagine two crypto holders. One made millions through lucky timing on a memecoin and spends most days scrolling charts, seeking the next hit. They've no estate plan, poor operational security, and little idea of how to translate their assets into usable structure. The second has half the portfolio value but a long-view orientation. They've integrated self-custody, split key recovery, modest fiat diversification, tax awareness, and education protocols for dependents. *Who is actually wealthier?*

This is not a moral judgement—it's a practical one. Because in the decentralised economy, you are your own bank, your own vault, your own fiduciary. The decisions you make don't just affect you—they cascade into your relationships, your psychological state, and the systems you leave behind. And when the market crashes—which it inevitably will—the difference between riches and wealth becomes painfully visible. *Riches evaporate. Wealth adjusts.*

It's worth acknowledging how hard it is to hold this distinction in real-time. The platforms we use reward engagement, not reflection. Price movements hit faster than reasoning. Communities celebrate loud wins more than quiet thinking. But this is why inner frameworks matter. You need your own north star. You need an internal system for distinguishing between signal and seduction. *Without that, you're not building wealth—you're riding waves you don't control.*

Ultimately, this chapter invites a reframing not just of ambition, but of identity. Who are you becoming through your financial practice? Are you cultivating patience, clarity, and competence—or are you reinforcing distraction, envy, and reaction? Wealth-building isn't simply a result of what you earn. It's a reflection of what you *prioritise.* It's about aligning capital with values, time with intention, risk with understanding.

This is the new calculus of decentralised living: not how fast can you grow, but how *deeply* can you anchor? Not how much can you earn this month, but how *long* can you last across cycles? Not what's trending, but what's *transferable* to future generations. Crypto is not a slot machine. It's a sovereignty toolkit. And if you treat it accordingly, you may not become the richest person in the feed—but you just might become the *wealthiest one in the room.*

Crypto as Legacy, Not Lottery:

It is tempting to view cryptocurrency as a mechanism for instant elevation—an escape hatch from economic limitations, or a one-click antidote to decades of traditional financial inertia. The culture surrounding it often reinforces this narrative: viral headlines of overnight gains, charts that resemble rocket launches, and influencer-driven FOMO loops. But this is not investment; it is theatre. *Crypto should be treated less like a lottery ticket and more like an inheritance strategy.* The difference is not only practical—it is philosophical. It reorients the conversation from extraction to continuity, from speculation to stewardship.

Wealth, to be meaningful across time, must be transmissible. Historically, land, art, businesses, and gold served this purpose: assets that could persist beyond the original owner and continue generating utility or significance for others. Bitcoin and other decentralised assets now join this lineage—but only if holders choose to treat them accordingly. *The digital nature of crypto does not exempt it from legacy planning; it demands more of it.*

Unlike traditional investments, crypto assets can be lost permanently with no recourse. There is no "forgot password" button for private keys. No bank manager to call. No probate lawyer with a ledger. What you do not structure for others, they cannot access. This is a radical kind of responsibility. It makes estate planning not a bureaucratic afterthought, but a moral act of foresight. You are not merely holding wealth—you are curating access to it. You are designing inheritance systems.

This makes crypto's ethos of self-custody a double-edged sword. On one hand, it offers sovereignty. On the other, it introduces existential fragility. A 24-word seed phrase stored improperly—or worse, not at all—can erase generations of effort. There are families who have lost millions because a single point of failure was never addressed. In this light, responsible crypto ownership is not just personal diligence; it is *intergenerational integrity.*

To treat crypto as a legacy asset requires an entirely different mental model. It is not about price charts; it's about *timeline charts.* How many market cycles do you want your holdings to endure? Can your capital outlive you, outlast regulations, and function across jurisdictions? These are questions traditionally reserved for trusts and endowments. Now, they belong to anyone with a hardware wallet. *Crypto compresses access to institutional-grade capital mechanics into everyday hands. But with that power comes a new demand: design your system, or default to fragility.*

Consider a thought experiment. Imagine your grandchildren inherit your portfolio. Can they read it? Can they understand your reasoning, the logic behind your allocations, the values you prioritised? Or are they left with a scatter of tokens, half-held passwords, and no narrative continuity? The assets themselves matter less than the *framing* of those assets. Legacy is not just what you leave, but *how you equip others to continue with it.*

This is why estate planning for crypto must move beyond legal compliance and become a form of personal authorship. You are writing the script for someone else's first interaction with wealth. Are you handing them a casino chip or a foundation? This involves more than key-sharing mechanisms. It includes educational layers—recorded explanations, curated reading lists, trust documents in plain English, and perhaps even simulation environments where heirs can practice decisions before the capital becomes theirs. *Legacy is pedagogy.*

It also requires emotional intelligence. Many crypto holders, particularly those who came into the space through volatility and earned gains under pressure, are reluctant to discuss their holdings with others. Sometimes this is fuelled by privacy, sometimes by fear of being perceived as greedy, sometimes by the mistaken belief that planning equals inviting decay. But refusing to talk about death does not delay it. Silence merely guarantees confusion. *If your financial system dies with you, it was never a system—it was a silo.*

This is not to suggest that all crypto must be frozen in conservative vaults. On the contrary, building legacy through crypto may still include active strategies: yield farming, validator operations, DAO participation, or venture allocation. The difference lies in scaffolding. The question is not "Is this risky?" but "Is this readable, explainable, repeatable?" That which cannot be explained cannot be handed down. That which relies on you being online 24/7 is not an asset—it is a job disguised as one. *Legacy detaches wealth from the necessity of your attention.*

Let us also acknowledge that treating crypto as legacy is a profound counter-cultural act. Most of the market thrives on dopamine, not duration. It is built to distract, not deepen. Yet the very volatility that tempts short-termism makes the case for durability. The cycles will punish those who overextend, over-leverage, or over-trade. But they will quietly reward those who build frameworks: cold storage solutions, multi-sig governance, redundancy protocols, geographic diversification. This is the difference between a volatile trader and a volatility-adapted investor.

Furthermore, crypto is not just a financial layer—it is a cultural one. The assets you hold also signal values. A wallet that contains climate-positive protocols, decentralised public goods tokens, or long-term infrastructure investments tells a different story than one filled with hype-driven collectibles. This isn't moralism; it's messaging. *Your wallet is a narrative device.* Future generations may not only inherit your holdings—they may be judged by them. What you back becomes part of what you're remembered for.

It is also vital to integrate legal and regulatory understanding. Despite the libertarian origins of crypto, responsible legacy planning involves engaging with formal estate structures: wills, trusts, succession clauses, powers of attorney. This may seem like a reversion to the old world, but it is not capitulation—it is *translation.* You are bridging decentralised assets into centralised systems so they can survive across time. The law is not your enemy; it is your infrastructure partner. A legacy built in code still needs interpretation in court.

We must also recognise the opportunity here for systemic change. Traditional estate planning has long been a domain of the wealthy—complicated, expensive, gate-kept. Crypto opens up the ability to pre-design multigenerational impact without needing intermediaries. Smart contract-based wills, programmable time-locked tokens, and decentralised family offices are no longer theoretical—they are increasingly operational. But they require intention. Technology does not automate wisdom.

In the end, legacy is not just what you pass on. It's the mindset you reinforce. A thoughtful crypto holder has the opportunity to teach those who follow them about patience, sovereignty, risk calibration, curiosity, and long-termism. You can help your children or heirs view capital not as an emotional crutch, but as a creative resource. Not as something to burn quickly, but as something to cultivate meaningfully. *Your portfolio is a curriculum in how to think about responsibility.*

So let us retire the lottery language. Let us stop reinforcing the fantasy of riches detached from responsibility. Crypto is not here to save us from reality; it is here to *force us to engage with it more fully*. And that includes planning for a time when we are no longer in the room, but our fingerprints remain on everything we've structured.

Legacy is not passive. It is crafted. It is the art of transferring not just assets, but *awareness*. Crypto gives us the tools. It is up to us to decide what kind of inheritance we are really leaving behind.

Time Horizons and the Power of Inaction:

Modern finance is animated by speed. High-frequency trades, instant news alerts, blinking dashboards, and meme-fuelled market manias all reinforce a single, implicit dogma: *if you're not doing something, you're falling behind.* This belief is not only widespread—it is intoxicating. Yet some of the most durable success stories in crypto and beyond reveal the opposite: *the investors who win across time are often those who did the least, most consistently.* In a world driven by reaction, inaction becomes a form of resistance—and more importantly, a powerful strategic tool.

This is not a defence of laziness. Nor is it a nostalgic yearning for "set and forget" models from an analogue era. Instead, it is a recalibration of where real returns are made: *not in the flicker of fast trades, but in the compound effects of long-term positioning.* The crypto space, for all its volatility and hype, is uniquely suited to reward those who build systems that thrive under time. What's needed is the ability to distinguish between noise and signal, motion and meaning, visibility and value.

It helps to start with the data. Numerous studies across traditional and crypto markets alike confirm the uncomfortable truth: the vast majority of traders underperform the assets they are trading. Fidelity once conducted an internal study to identify their most successful retail investors. The top performers? Clients who had forgotten they had accounts—or were deceased. The implication is not mystical. It's behavioural. *Doing less often protects you from your worst instincts.*

The psychological mechanisms are well-known but rarely internalised. Loss aversion, confirmation bias, recency bias, and the illusion of control combine to seduce intelligent people into over-activity. Every market dip feels personal. Every rally feels like a missed opportunity. The reflex is to intervene, even when the optimal strategy is to wait. This is not a failure of knowledge; it is a failure of design. *Inaction cannot be willed—it must be engineered.*

To that end, time horizons are not just calendar settings. They are philosophical commitments. To adopt a 10-year horizon in crypto is not merely to click a dropdown menu on a trading app. It is to actively reject a culture that equates urgency with wisdom. It is to develop a different relationship with volatility, one where price movements are no longer prompts for action, but inputs into a broader understanding of cycles, sentiment, and adoption curves. *Patience, properly structured, becomes a competitive advantage.*

Consider the structure of Bitcoin itself. Every four years, the halving reduces block rewards, slowly tightening the asset's emission schedule. This was not built for fast money. It was designed for people who could think in epochs, not quarters. Ethereum's transition to proof-of-stake embedded similar time-aligned features, rewarding validators who operate over months and years, not minutes. The underlying protocols are telling us something: *value, when decentralised, accrues to those who align with time, not against it.*

There is also a deeper irony at play. Much of the crypto world claims to resist legacy finance, yet mimics its most impulsive traits—day trading, performance-chasing, derivative obsession. But the truly revolutionary act in this space may not be radical experimentation—it may be strategic stillness. That is, *designing personal systems that do not require your constant presence to function effectively.*

This is not merely theory. Leading investors—from family offices to individual holders—are beginning to institutionalise these behaviours. Multi-sig wallets with restricted access during market volatility. Time-locked smart contracts that enforce cooling-off periods before asset transfers. Portfolio structures with tiered liquidity layers, ensuring that only a small percentage is exposed to near-term decision-making. These are not limitations; they are *discipline devices.*

In many ways, this is the evolution of the "barbell strategy"—holding a large portion in extremely safe, long-term assets, and a small percentage in high-risk, high-reward ventures. What's often overlooked is that *the success of the strategy depends less on what you buy, and more on how often you try to interfere with it.* The design must reward boredom. The investor must be allowed—encouraged, even—to forget they are investing.

But the pull to act is strong. It feels responsible. It feels rational. Doing nothing, by contrast, feels negligent—until you realise that *most market movements are noise wrapped in narrative.* Zoom out far enough, and most short-term drama vanishes into the statistical fog. And yet, many investors structure their lives as if each tweet, each chart wiggle, demands an existential reaction. This is not investing. It is emotional outsourcing.

To break this pattern, systems must be reoriented toward stability, not stimulation. This includes practical steps: limiting portfolio checks to scheduled intervals, automating dollar-cost averaging, using non-custodial protocols with staking rewards that disincentivise withdrawals. But it also includes inner work: redefining what success looks like. *If your benchmark is constant activity, you'll always feel behind. If your benchmark is time-aligned conviction, progress becomes silent but certain.*

One of the paradoxes of investing is that the most sophisticated systems often look unsophisticated from the outside. They appear static. They don't broadcast every move. They are not performance-art portfolios for public consumption. But they work. And they do so because they are built on the awareness that *compounding is a function of duration, not drama.*

This ethos is deeply countercultural, especially in crypto. But it is not new. The world's most enduring fortunes—from property dynasties to endowments—have been built by those who mastered the art of strategic inaction. Not apathy. Not avoidance. But the discipline to design decisions in advance, and the humility to let time do its work.

And perhaps most importantly, these systems are not only financial. They are emotional architectures. They reduce anxiety by reducing input overload. They free cognitive bandwidth by reducing unnecessary decision points. They allow you to reclaim energy that would otherwise be squandered on false urgency. *In this sense, financial stillness is also mental liberation.*

There is one final benefit worth naming: legacy. The fewer levers your system requires, the easier it is to transmit. A portfolio that needs daily adjustments is not a portfolio—it is a burden. But a system that runs quietly, that reflects values over volatility, can be inherited, understood, and adapted. It becomes not just an allocation of capital, but a philosophy of capital.

So the next time a headline screams for action, the market tugs at your instinct to respond, or the timeline spins with panic and euphoria, pause. Ask not what the market is doing today. Ask what your system is designed to do across decades. *Sometimes, the greatest act of skill is the act you never perform.*

The future belongs to those who can think across time, act with restraint, and design for silence. Inaction is not the absence of intelligence—it is its highest expression.

Teaching the Next Generation:

When most people speak about crypto as "the future," they are rarely speaking to the future. Institutional conversations about blockchain adoption, decentralised finance, and tokenised value systems are still overwhelmingly focused on adult stakeholders—investors, regulators, founders, policymakers. Yet, if we accept that crypto is not just a new financial asset but a structural shift in how value is stored, signalled, and transmitted, then the most vital audience isn't the present—it's the inheritors of what we build. Teaching the next generation is not just about giving them access to wallets or private keys. It's about transmitting the values, models, and mental scaffolding necessary to navigate a decentralised future with wisdom, not just wealth.

The starting point is simple but often overlooked: financial systems are cultural systems. Every ledger encodes a worldview. A traditional bank account teaches deference to authority and institutional trust. A crypto wallet, by contrast, introduces autonomy, personal responsibility, and the permanence of public action. This difference is not superficial—it is epistemological. And just as we wouldn't hand a child a power tool without guidance, we shouldn't hand them a blockchain address without context. *Crypto fluency must begin with crypto philosophy.* That includes hard conversations about privacy, permanence, risk, and control—conversations too often skipped in the rush to onboard.

The mistake many make is to treat crypto education as a purely technical task: teaching how to use a wallet, how to avoid scams, how to read a transaction hash. These are necessary but insufficient. True transmission involves teaching how to *think* about crypto. Why self-custody matters. What it means to hold assets no state can seize. How consensus mechanisms mirror human coordination dilemmas. How anonymity and transparency coexist in complex tension. These are not tutorials. They are worldview shifts. They require storytelling, analogies, critical inquiry—not just documentation and interfaces.

One promising approach is to frame crypto not as an asset class but as an inheritance model. Not what you invest in, but what you *pass on.* This reorientation elevates the conversation from profit to purpose. A well-designed inheritance is not a list of coins in cold storage; it's a logic for navigating uncertainty, a set of values encoded into protocols, an approach to thinking probabilistically across time. If your child receives your crypto without your frameworks, they inherit tools without training. And in this system, tools without training are liabilities.

Legacy in this context demands more than legal documentation—it demands pedagogical design. A trust fund built in a decentralised system can't rely on lawyers and vaults. It requires smart contracts, custody schemes, and social recovery mechanisms that can outlive the founder. That means involving your family or community in the logic of these systems while you're still around to explain them. *Estate planning in crypto is not a legal event—it's a learning process.* It unfolds not in the final years of life, but in the prime of it.

Consider the architecture of a family crypto vault. Rather than naming a single heir, one could construct a multi-signature wallet governed by a quorum of trusted individuals. Access protocols could require intergenerational cooperation—perhaps a parent and two children must jointly sign to unlock funds. But more than security, this mechanism encodes a lesson: *coordination is the cost of control.* It forces engagement, dialogue, mutual trust. These become part of the legacy itself—not just the assets, but the operating procedures.

Passing on crypto also means teaching what *not* to do. This includes familiarising the next generation with the psychological traps of volatility, the allure of short-termism, the social pressure to perform wealth online. If you've learned to sit through bear markets, avoid emotional trading, and filter signal from noise, these are not just personal skills—they are pedagogical assets. Share the losses. Share the regrets. Share the charts you watched instead of acting. These stories teach better than spreadsheets ever could. *Transparency in your own experience is the curriculum your family actually remembers.*

The educational systems that currently exist are poorly equipped to take up this mantle. Most schools still treat personal finance as a marginal topic, let alone crypto literacy. This creates an opportunity—and a responsibility—for families, communities, and decentralised networks to fill the gap. It may start with small actions:

encouraging a teenager to set up a non-custodial wallet, co-investing in a project together, or having regular family debriefs on crypto news and narratives. The goal is not early trading. It's early thinking. *The earlier someone learns to contextualise risk, responsibility, and protocol-level trust, the more resilient their financial worldview becomes.*

Some may argue that crypto is too complex or too volatile for young people. But this underestimates both the capacity of the learner and the responsibility of the teacher. Complexity is not a barrier—it's an invitation. Children are not confused by cryptographic primitives or economic game theory because they're "too abstract." They're confused when those abstractions are poorly explained. The job is not to simplify crypto into cartoon versions of coins and tokens. The job is to respect young minds enough to give them clarity. *Teaching crypto well is teaching critical thinking under uncertainty.* And this is a skill for life, not just for markets.

Another often missed dimension is *values transfer.* What are you actually hoping your crypto assets represent? Sovereignty? Philanthropy? Intergenerational resilience? Teaching the next generation means clarifying not just how to hold wealth, but *why.* A digital asset held in cold storage without purpose is no different than buried treasure. But one held with explicit intention—supporting causes, funding experiments, underwriting community efforts—becomes a signal of values. Teach not just the mechanics of staking, swapping, and securing, but the ethics of participation. How does one evaluate a token beyond its price? How should a person act when holding outsized influence in a DAO? When is selling a betrayal of mission? These are the conversations that define legacy.

One of the richest opportunities lies in collaborative design. Invite your children or mentees into the architecture of the wallet itself. Ask: what should go in here, and why? What tokens reflect our shared values? What protocols align with our principles? What naming conventions or NFT collections will tell our story when we're not around? This is not abstract theorising—it's codified identity. *Crypto tools allow us to write our philosophy into software. We should do so consciously, and teach others to do the same.*

The long arc of wealth is not accumulation—it is transmission. And crypto, for all its disruptions, brings us back to something ancient: the act of equipping the next generation not with answers, but with orientation. In a decentralised world, that orientation must be internal. Self-custody is not just about private keys; it's about having the confidence to hold your own logic, your own frameworks, your own sovereignty—even in the face of noise. Teaching this mindset is the real inheritance.

If we want the next generation to treat crypto not as a game or a gamble but as a foundation for autonomy, coordination, and integrity, then we must model those values ourselves. We must teach not just how to navigate systems, but how to shape them. Not just how to protect wealth, but how to *understand what it's for.* And above all, we must understand that every conversation, every decision, every design choice in our own crypto lives is a lesson—whether we realise it or not. Better, then, to be intentional.

We do not pass on wealth. We pass on wisdom wrapped in wealth. The asset is secondary. The understanding is primary. And the only enduring store of value is the thinking that survives us.

Chapter 8
Tools of the New Wealth Architect

Rewrite the following article to pass AI-detection tools while retaining its professional, intellectually engaging, and authoritative tone.

Rephrase and restructure the content to feel human-authored, with a writing style that reflects the subtle imperfections and expressive flow of a skilled writer.

Specifically: – Vary sentence structures, paragraph rhythms, and transition choices to avoid algorithmic patterns

– Introduce occasional conversational touches or rhetorical asides where appropriate

– Make subtle word choices or phrase shifts that sound natural but aren't statistically predictable

– Avoid "perfectly smooth" sentence-to-sentence transitions—a little friction is more human

– Maintain the original meaning, flow, facts, and paragraphing

– Do not simplify or summarise—this is not a paraphrasing task, but a creative re-authorship

– Use British English conventions

– Ensure the result still reads like it was written by a seasoned nonfiction writer with intellectual and emotional depth

Output only the reworked article text. No explanations. No headers. No setup language

The crypto space does not reward passivity—it invites participation. But not all participation is created equal. In the heat of volatility and the noise of endless innovation, the investor or builder who survives—and thrives—is not necessarily the one who knows the most, moves the fastest, or bets the biggest. It's the one who designs their thinking. The one who builds systems not just of capital allocation, but of psychological resilience and strategic clarity. This chapter is about becoming that person. It is about developing the intellectual infrastructure and behavioural protocols that separate the distracted speculator from the intentional wealth architect.

At its core, the shift we're exploring is from reaction to ritual. The typical crypto participant operates in a state of alert—a constant scanning of headlines, token launches, airdrops, governance proposals, protocol shifts. This mode may feel productive, even necessary. But it's a trap. It encourages short time horizons, fragmented attention, and emotion-driven decisions. The architect, by contrast, operates from a place of clarity. They create conditions where the most important decisions are not made in the moment—they're made once, upstream, and embedded into systems. They design habits that protect their attention, rules that filter their engagement, and rituals that convert information into insight.

Consider automations—not just as convenience tools, but as philosophical commitments. A recurring buy order, for example, is not merely a function of time or cash flow. It is a declaration: I believe in long-term compounding more than my ability to time the market. Similarly, a scheduled portfolio rebalancing mechanism isn't just portfolio hygiene—it's a commitment to discipline over drama. These small acts encode conviction, and more importantly, they free the mind. Reducing decision fatigue is not a productivity hack—it's a psychological moat. In a landscape of constant novelty, the ability to act without overthinking becomes a competitive advantage.

But this advantage is only sustainable if it's paired with robust internal filters. This is where most people fail. The crypto world does not suffer from a scarcity of opportunity—it suffers from a surplus of distraction. Every week brings a new layer-2, a new narrative, a new tokenomics model, a new "must-read" thread. The unfiltered mind will chase them all. The architect builds a gate. They develop a taxonomy of relevance: What fits my thesis? What aligns with my values? What can I actually understand deeply enough to justify engagement? Without these filters, even the most sophisticated investor will eventually revert to pattern-matching and performance-chasing. And in this market, chasing is the beginning of losing.

This brings us to perhaps the most underutilised yet high-leverage tool of all: the crypto journal. Not a blog. Not a public thread. A private, disciplined record of decisions, thoughts, and emotions. When did you buy? Why? What assumptions did you make? What signals did you trust—or ignore? What did you feel before and after? These entries form the raw material for feedback loops. They allow for second-order learning. Over time, you see your own mind on paper: your biases, your blind spots, your growth. A well-kept crypto journal is not a diary—it's a dataset of the self.

And unlike a portfolio tracker, it captures what numbers never can: the context of your choices. The market may be irrational, but your reactions don't have to be. Most people look back on trades with only one lens—profit or loss. But that view is sterile. A well-structured journal lets you evaluate a decision on quality, not just outcome. Did you follow your framework? Did you exit based on signal or noise? Were you reactive or deliberate? This is the kind of self-inquiry that compounds—not just your wealth, but your wisdom.

Of course, all of this assumes that you've taken the time to define your own frameworks. And that's where architecture becomes art. There is no universal crypto philosophy. What works for one person may be poison to another. The key is not to follow the most popular model, but to author your own. To know whether you are a builder or an allocator. To understand your tolerance for volatility, your need for liquidity, your beliefs about technology and governance. To write these into principles—not just ideas in your head, but visible, testable, challengeable rules. Wealth, in this context, is not just a number. It's a structure of decisions made over time, with consistency and care.

What this chapter offers, then, is not just advice. It's a blueprint. We will walk through how to set up the systems that allow for clarity amidst chaos. We will discuss how to turn healthy behaviours into automated flows—so your discipline doesn't rely on daily willpower. We will examine how to spot and resist "shiny object syndrome"—not just as a distraction, but as a threat to your compounded returns. And we'll explore how to build a living record of your evolution as an investor, thinker, and sovereign participant in a decentralised world.

This is the quiet work—the work no one tweets about, the processes hidden behind every wise portfolio and every long-term success. But it is precisely this hidden scaffolding that makes the difference. A well-designed system will outperform a brilliant but erratic mind over any meaningful time horizon. And in a space where narratives shift hourly, that kind of edge is priceless.

What we are ultimately building here is a new kind of literacy. Not just financial, not just technological—but behavioural and philosophical. The literacy to operate in decentralised systems without being consumed by them. The literacy to design your interface with chaos. This chapter is your invitation to stop improvising and start engineering. To stop reacting and start architecting. Because the future belongs not to those who know the most, but to those who have built the tools to think clearly when others cannot.

Building a Personal Tech Stack

At a glance, assembling your crypto toolset might seem like a purely technical task—choose a wallet, plug in a dashboard, automate your yield. But treated thoughtfully, it becomes something else entirely: a practice in self-mastery. The tools we use shape not only our decisions but our disposition. They encode our values, enforce our limits, reflect our beliefs about time, trust, and sovereignty. In a decentralised world where infrastructure is personal, *your tech stack is no longer just an operational layer—it is an expression of identity.*

This chapter is not about listing tools. It's about reframing your entire approach to tooling as intentional architecture. Think of it as building an exoskeleton for your judgement. In traditional finance, your bank decides how you interact with money. In crypto, *you decide what you see, what you secure, and what you automate.* That autonomy is powerful—but also dangerous. Without deliberate curation, the very tools meant to empower can overwhelm. Just as a cluttered mind leads to reactive decisions, a chaotic tool stack leads to scattered strategy. So we begin with a question: *what kind of thinker do you want to be in this system?*

Every technology choice should flow from that answer.

Start with security—not as paranoia, but as philosophy. A hardware wallet, properly configured, is not simply a device. It is *a boundary between signal and catastrophe.* Choosing to custody your keys offline is not just risk management—it is a commitment to independence. It's saying: I do not outsource my sovereignty. The physicality of a Ledger or Trezor introduces friction that matters. That friction forces reflection. Hot wallets may offer convenience, but convenience is not neutral—it shapes behaviour. The easier it is to transact, the easier it is to panic. Cold storage introduces a pause, and that pause is often the margin between regret and restraint.

But security without visibility is just a bunker. To act with clarity, you must be able to see—not just your assets, but your exposures, your flows, your yield paths, your slippage. An analytics dashboard is not merely a performance tracker; it is your map. Platforms like DeBank, Zapper, or Rotki (especially when run locally) offer a consolidated view across protocols, chains, and wallets. But more importantly, they allow you to *construct your own mental model of your financial terrain.* That's crucial, because decentralised finance does not provide a single source of truth. You must define what metrics matter to you. Is it net worth? APY? Protocol risk? Gas fees? Wallet hygiene? Without clarity on the signal, you will drown in noise.

Consider automation next. Not as laziness, but as leverage. In a volatile, composable ecosystem, manual execution is a liability. Tools like Gnosis Safe, Gelato, or Yearn enable structured, conditional, and repeatable strategies. But again, the technology is only as strong as the thinking behind it. Automating a bad decision just makes the mistake faster. The question is: *what behaviours are you trying to lock in?* For some, it's dollar-cost averaging. For others, it's rebalancing between assets, or migrating yield based on thresholds. Each automation is a vote for consistency over spontaneity. *Systems outperform moods*. When you automate, you aren't delegating to code—you're protecting yourself from yourself.

This reframing matters because most people approach tooling reactively. They discover tools the way they discover tokens: through Twitter threads, Discord tips, and market euphoria. But that discovery model produces fragmentation. A dashboard here, a wallet there, an app that only works on one chain, another that doesn't support hardware wallets. Before long, their stack reflects the industry's chaos rather than their own clarity. *You are not your MetaMask popups*. A coherent toolset should reduce decision fatigue, not introduce new confusion. It should be a curated environment that reflects your cognitive style, not the industry's tempo.

Let's go deeper. Beyond wallets and dashboards lies an under-discussed layer of tooling: introspective infrastructure. This includes tools like journaling apps, behavioural trackers, and financial diaries. At first glance, these seem peripheral. But if the goal is mastery—not just performance—then this layer is essential. It is the only part of your stack that captures *why* you did something, not just *what*. Most investors track prices, few track mindset. Most monitor ROI, few monitor regret. But in crypto, where volatility weaponises emotion, *your internal data is often more actionable than market data*.

A simple journaling prompt after every major action—buy, sell, stake, unstake, bridge, vote—can reveal more over time than any chart. What were you feeling? What was your thesis? What was the counterargument? Would you take this action again under the same conditions? These reflections don't need to be long. But when aggregated, they form an archive of your evolution as a decision-maker. They help you diagnose your own edge—not just in what you know, but in *how you think under pressure*. No hardware wallet can secure that. Only a well-maintained awareness stack can.

Even community-based tooling deserves attention. Who are your information nodes? What Discord servers, Telegram groups, newsletters, or DAOs inform your thinking? Your information diet is part of your stack. Consuming five DeFi threads per day may feel like research. But is it? Most people are building *mental noise*, not mental models. A high-signal feed is not necessarily one with the most alpha leaks. It's one that aligns with your time horizon, risk profile, and ideological integrity. In a world obsessed with "firsts"—first to mint, first to ape, first to exit—the wise investor optimises for *filters*, not *feeds*.

The tech stack you build will influence your relationship to risk, control, and pace. Some stacks push you to act constantly, to chase trends, to refresh dashboards compulsively. Others encourage patience, perspective, and principled engagement. The best stack is not the one with the most tools—it's the one with the fewest distractions. Every added tool should serve a purpose you can articulate. If it doesn't, it becomes a liability, not an asset. *Tool bloat is mental bloat.* Clean systems invite clean thinking.

Critically, this is not a one-time build. Your stack will evolve. As protocols mature, as threats shift, as your financial situation changes, so too should your infrastructure. That adaptability is healthy. But the changes should be driven by you—not by hype, not by peers, and not by FOMO. Periodically audit your stack. What's still serving you? What's just legacy clutter? What do you actually understand deeply, and what are you blindly trusting? *The more complex your tooling becomes, the more important it is to regain simplicity in strategy.*

There is one final layer that rarely gets acknowledged: *aesthetics*. The tools you use every day shape how you feel about your practice. A clean UI, an elegant UX, an interface that respects your time—these are not luxuries. They are cues. They remind you that your wealth strategy is not a desperate sprint but a composed craft. Your stack should invite clarity, not anxiety. A frictionless experience isn't just convenient—it's instructive. It teaches your nervous system to associate investing not with stress, but with stewardship.

To master crypto, you must master your tools. But mastery here does not mean encyclopaedic knowledge. It means *alignment between your technology and your temperament.* Tools are not neutral. They reflect choices—about what to secure, what to prioritise, what to see, and what to ignore. A personal tech stack is not a kit. It is a mirror. And when built intentionally, it reflects back not just your portfolio—but your philosophy.

"Automations and Rituals"

The most sophisticated investors don't make more decisions than everyone else—they make fewer. They build systems that protect them from noise, automate their best thinking, and remove themselves from the tyranny of the moment. In a financial landscape that is increasingly fast, fragmented, and emotionally charged, *discipline is not enough.* What matters is *structured discipline*—the kind enforced not by willpower, but by design.

This is where automation and ritual intersect. Automation absorbs complexity. Ritual absorbs volatility. Together, they form a protective architecture for both wealth and mind. In the decentralised economy, where the traditional scaffolding of banks and institutions is replaced by protocols and user-defined pathways, your behavioural infrastructure *is* your financial infrastructure. The decisions you don't have to make are often the ones that keep your strategy intact.

Take dollar-cost averaging (DCA) as an illustrative baseline. On the surface, it's a simple technique: allocate a fixed amount of money into an asset at regular intervals, regardless of price. But underneath lies something deeper: *a philosophy of detachment from short-term noise.* DCA removes the psychological load of timing the market, replacing guesswork with rhythm. In the crypto context—where markets move 24/7 and attention is a scarce commodity—this kind of automation becomes less about mechanics and more about mental hygiene. You are outsourcing decision-making not to laziness, but to *principled constraint.*

Consider further the case of auto-staking, auto-rebalancing, or programmed portfolio shifts through tools like DeFi Smart Accounts, Gnosis Safe, or protocols like Yearn, Beefy, or Sommelier. These aren't simply convenience features—they are behavioural contracts. You are telling the system: "Protect me from my lesser self." When you automate a rebalance based on volatility thresholds rather than gut feeling, you're institutionalising prudence. When you set a yield route that diverts earnings into long-term assets or liquidity positions, you are rehearsing long-term thinking, again and again, without needing to debate it each time.

Rituals, though often undervalued in the rationalist framing of finance, serve a different but equally important function. Where automations are machines of consistency, rituals are *containers for clarity*. They bring deliberate consciousness to the parts of investing that resist codification. For example, reviewing your portfolio every Sunday—not to trade, but to reflect—is a ritual. Reading a newsletter or on-chain data report before making any new investment, regardless of sentiment, is a ritual. Taking thirty minutes to journal your emotional state after a sharp drawdown—that, too, is ritual. These practices are not mechanical, but they are not optional either. They create mental buffers. *They slow down the speed of reactivity just enough to enable perspective.*

There is a common misconception that more decisions equal better results. But crypto markets, with their speed and infinite surface area, reward restraint far more than hyperactivity. Most poor outcomes stem not from bad information, but from *context collapse*—the inability to make coherent decisions in a high-stimulation environment. Automation solves for overaction. Ritual solves for disorientation. Together, they return agency to the investor. They preserve energy for the decisions that matter most—and hard-code away the ones that should never be made impulsively.

Let's bring in a practical example. Suppose an investor allocates across several stablecoin yield platforms and volatile crypto assets. Without systematised behaviours, the temptation to chase higher returns with each new protocol becomes constant. However, if the investor sets parameters—such as "no yield migrations more than once per month" or "cap stablecoin reallocation to 20% of yield"—and enforces these via a dashboard like DeFi Saver or a multisig, they shift from reactive to intentional. These rules can be embedded into executional workflows. They're not just decisions—they're embedded preferences.

This principle of embedding extends beyond financial tools. It applies to cognitive architecture as well. How you start your day, what you check first, what triggers your trade ideas—these are all behaviours that either serve your long-term thinking or sabotage it. For instance, if the first thing you do in the morning is open your wallet tracker, you've already primed yourself to think about your identity in terms of price. A more powerful ritual might be: first read your own investment thesis. Reconnect to why you hold what you hold. That orientation shift changes the lens through which you interpret the data you're about to see. *Clarity before stimulus—that is a strategic posture.*

Too often, automation is framed in coldly technical terms—scripts, smart contracts, bots. But the higher-order use of automation is as a *substitute for willpower.* Not because you lack discipline, but because you understand its limits. Human attention is finite. Human patience is fragile. Smart investors don't try to be superhuman—they build systems that make good behaviour effortless and bad behaviour difficult. Think of it this way: would you rather depend on your motivation to remember to rebalance every quarter, or have a smart contract execute it for you? Would you rather hope you don't panic during a crash, or design a rule that locks you out of trades when volatility spikes? *Good automation is behavioural insurance.*

Even rituals can be partially automated. For example, setting a recurring calendar reminder to review your net exposure on the first of every month. Or tagging major wallet movements with a required annotation field: "What is the intent behind this transaction?" These friction points seem minor, but they function like circuit breakers. They insert pause. And that pause creates space for reflection—a critical scarce resource in crypto.

To be clear, not everything should be automated. Not every decision benefits from being outsourced to rules or scripts. The role of automation is to reduce friction in known-good behaviours, not to eliminate strategy altogether. There must still be space for discretion, especially in navigating emergent risks or opportunities. But the paradox is that by automating the *right things*, you *earn the bandwidth* to be present for the ambiguous ones. *Automated discipline frees up strategic cognition.*

Automation and ritual are also scalable. As your portfolio grows, or as you take on the responsibility of managing assets for others—whether in a DAO, syndicate, or family context—the ability to codify behaviour into repeatable systems becomes critical. It's no longer just about what *you* believe. It's about what the system enforces. If a friend inherits your setup, would they inherit a mess of untracked links and scattered positions—or a clear, replicable structure with built-in rules? This is where automation becomes not just protective, but *transmissive.* It lets wisdom persist beyond context.

Let's zoom out. What this subchapter ultimately invites is a redefinition of strategy. Strategy is not merely *what* you aim to do—it is *how consistently you can behave under pressure.* The best strategies collapse under emotional load if not insulated by process. You may believe in long-term holding, but if you're checking prices every hour and rebalancing every week, your behaviour is out of sync with your belief. That misalignment is costly—not just financially, but cognitively. It generates decision fatigue, self-doubt, and stress. Systems heal that dissonance. They are how you act in line with your values *even when your emotions rebel.*

In a market defined by speed, the edge belongs to those who master slow thinking. But slowness cannot be sustained through force of will alone. It must be *engineered.* And that is the real promise of automations and rituals: they allow you to move at the speed of principle, not the speed of panic. They are the silent, stubborn scaffolding of serious investing. Invisible when working, obvious when absent. Underappreciated, yet foundational.

To invest well in crypto—or any domain of volatility—is not just a matter of insight, but of endurance. And endurance is not achieved by running faster. It's achieved by reducing drag. Drag from doubt, distraction, and decision clutter. Systems remove that drag. And in doing so, they let your best thinking compound over time.

What you automate is what you prioritise. What you ritualise is what you respect. Everything else is wishful thinking.

Avoiding Shiny Object Syndrome:

Nothing burns through capital faster than the illusion of opportunity. In the crypto economy—where new tokens launch daily, protocols pivot weekly, and influencers amplify micro-narratives hourly—the temptation to chase novelty is not a bug, it's the feature. Shiny Object Syndrome (SOS) is not a sign of personal weakness; it is a predictable response to a structurally over-stimulated market. The challenge is not avoiding distraction once—it's developing a reliable filter so you can ignore 98% of noise *consistently*, without feeling like you're missing out.

At its core, SOS is a breakdown in focus driven by informational overload. It thrives in environments where velocity outpaces verification. The faster something appears, the less time one has to interrogate its foundations—and paradoxically, the more urgent it feels to act. This dynamic exploits both our biology and our biases: novelty triggers dopamine; scarcity triggers urgency; complexity flatters our intelligence. Combine those, and you get a psychological trap disguised as a "hot opportunity."

What makes crypto uniquely vulnerable to this phenomenon is the permissionless nature of innovation. In traditional finance or technology sectors, gatekeepers screen what reaches the public—via regulatory hurdles, institutional filtering, or market readiness. In crypto, a new token can go from whitepaper to exchange listing in 72 hours. Anyone with a compelling narrative and a liquidity pool can command attention. This makes the market fertile ground for experimentation, but also for entropy. Without personal filters, the environment becomes untradeable—not because of lack of quality, but because of excess quantity.

So the question becomes: how do you architect a mindset and toolkit that resists distraction without defaulting to cynicism? How do you cultivate discernment—not by closing your mind, but by refining your attention?

The answer starts with *anchoring to purpose.* Every investor, consciously or not, has a thesis: a set of beliefs about what kinds of assets will outperform over time, and why. Yet in practice, few articulate this thesis in explicit, testable terms. Instead, they operate from vague instincts—"I like this team," or "It's early in the cycle"—which offer no resistance against the gravitational pull of newness. A well-formed thesis functions like a membrane: it lets through what aligns and filters out what distracts. If you can't explain what kind of projects *should* matter to your strategy, then *everything* can feel relevant—and relevance is the first step toward overreach.

To make this practical, consider a few framing questions:
– What is my time horizon? (Am I seeking short-term liquidity or long-term infrastructure exposure?)
– What layer of the stack am I focused on? (Base layer chains? Application protocols? Consumer crypto?)
– What kind of risk am I structurally willing to take? (Smart contract risk? Regulatory risk? Illiquidity risk?)
– What behaviours am I trying to reward in my portfolio? (Stability? Growth? Optionality?)

These aren't just preferences—they are filters. And once defined, they become powerful constraints. They reduce your susceptibility to distraction not by eliminating curiosity, but by giving it direction.

Beyond strategic filters, investors need *tactical friction.* In a market designed for hyper-speed, it's dangerous to be able to act on impulse with a single click. One of the simplest interventions is time-based gating: require a 24-hour cooling-off period before entering any new position. During that window, review the project not just for fundamentals, but for *fit.* Ask: "Would I still be interested if the price didn't move for six months?" or "Would I be willing to double down if it dropped 50% tomorrow?" These are pressure tests. They reveal whether you're investing from thesis or FOMO.

Another approach is mental categorisation. Not all ideas need to go into the portfolio. Some are for watching, some for learning, others for discarding. Create tiers. Your primary allocation should remain thesis-driven. Secondary ideas can sit in a sandbox—tracked, researched, but not acted upon until a threshold is met (e.g. product launch, audit completion, key partnership). This keeps curiosity alive without polluting conviction.

There's also a deeper level of analysis required: *what exactly is being sold?* Often, the surface-level offering is not the product—it's the narrative. A project might pitch itself as "the future of decentralised media," but is the real pitch an inflationary token with staking incentives and no path to revenue? Being able to separate storytelling from substance is a learned skill. It requires slow reading, questioning assumptions, and decoding incentives.

Consider the wave of "modular blockchains" or "AI-integrated DeFi" that capture headlines. While many of these may hold merit, they often arrive with thin technical depth and thick promotional polish. They are optimised for attention, not execution. The antidote is to step back from the pitch and ask: *what problem is this actually solving? Is the tech uniquely suited to solve it? Is there a real user base—or just speculative liquidity?* When attention is the currency, discernment is the arbitrage.

One powerful tool for resisting SOS is maintaining an *anti-portfolio.* This is a list of projects you chose *not* to invest in, and why. Over time, this log becomes a mirror of your thinking. It exposes whether your filters are too tight, too loose, or simply misaligned with outcomes. More importantly, it turns regret into data. Every missed opportunity is a potential refinement, not a reason to abandon discipline. A thoughtful anti-portfolio makes you less reactive. It reminds you that success in investing is not about catching every wave—it's about riding the ones that align with your craft.

We also must address the emotional layer. Much of SOS is fuelled by a deep discomfort with stillness. Watching others post gains, seeing new charts erupt on Twitter, hearing about "the next 100x" on Discord—these aren't just distractions, they are threats to identity. They whisper: *You're being left behind. You're not moving fast enough.* And the antidote to this is not more information. It is internal orientation. A clear sense of personal values. Why are you in crypto? What are you building? What are you protecting? *The more clearly you define success on your own terms, the less vulnerable you are to other people's excitement.*

Discipline is often mischaracterised as restraint. But true discipline is *clarity in action.* It is the ability to say no confidently because you've

– **Date and time of the decision.** Time stamps help connect market context (macro news, asset prices, funding rates) to internal context (stress, overconfidence, fear of missing out).
– **Asset or protocol involved.** Not just "Bought ETH," but *what chain, what purpose, what layer of conviction?*
– **Reasoning.** What information were you acting on? Was it technical analysis? A whitepaper? A tweet? A friend's tip? Note the source and why it felt credible.
– **Emotional state.** Were you excited, anxious, bored? Tracking emotional states reveals recurring patterns—such as impulsivity during boredom or risk-seeking when up significantly.
– **Expectation.** What did you think would happen? Not in vague terms like "moon" or "pump," but concrete forecasts: "Expecting 20% move in 2 weeks due to XYZ catalyst."
– **Exit plan.** Did you define one? Or were you entering with the intention of "figuring it out later"?

Captured over time, this kind of information is revelatory. You'll begin to notice how often you act without a plan, how rarely your expectations match reality, how certain emotions precede certain types of trades. This transforms your trading from reactive to reflective. It elevates you from participant to practitioner.

Importantly, journaling should not be reserved for major trades or portfolio overhauls. *The true value emerges when you log the small, routine decisions—the ones that feel unremarkable in the moment but compound over time.* That rushed swap at midnight. That new yield farm you "just tried for fun." That DCA you set and forgot. These are the micro-behaviours that, aggregated, define the architecture of your portfolio—and often, your returns.

Digital tools make this practice frictionless. A private Notion dashboard, a tagged Evernote notebook, even a simple encrypted text file. The medium matters less than the consistency. What you're building is a private ledger—not just of transactions, but of thinking. Over time, it becomes a chronicle of your evolution as an investor. A written record of not only *what* you did, but *how* you think.

What distinguishes a high-performing investor from a reckless one is not necessarily intelligence—it's the ability to close feedback loops. Without a journal, you repeat mistakes hidden beneath different assets. You blame volatility for what was actually poor reasoning. You think you're growing because you're learning new jargon, but you're not integrating experience. A journal enforces *iteration.* It turns experience into insight.

There is also a deeper benefit. In crypto, decisions are rarely made in isolation. Every allocation is nested within a broader set of beliefs—about decentralisation, sovereignty, technology, and the future of value. When you write regularly, your worldview becomes visible. You realise, for example, that you invest more confidently in projects that align with your values, not just your models. That your scepticism around governance tokens stems not from ignorance, but from a principled concern about voter incentives. Journaling helps you notice when your portfolio drifts away from your philosophy.

It also reveals meta-patterns. Do you panic sell during downturns, or do you overbuy during hype cycles? Do you research less when the market is up? Do you get more opinionated the more time you spend on Twitter? These behavioural insights are the raw material of mastery. No amount of alpha matters if your psychology remains unexamined.

The journal also acts as a hedge against false narratives—both internal and external. Crypto history is full of revisionism. People forget the level of conviction they had in failing projects. They rewrite their role in winners. Over time, this distorts your sense of agency. A journal provides resistance. It says: *this is what you actually thought, before the outcome coloured it.* That's the only reliable reference point for learning.

Furthermore, journaling decentralises your growth. Most people wait for external validation—returns, accolades, community clout—to believe they're improving. But a journal creates an internal metric: *Am I reasoning better? Am I more precise in my thinking? Am I more consistent in my execution?* It reorients your focus from outcomes to process. This is what it means to think like a long-term operator rather than a short-term speculator.

Beyond individual performance, the journal becomes an artefact. In years to come, your entries will reflect not just market cycles, but historical insight. What it felt like to experience the merge. The chaos of a bear market bottom. The emergence of new primitives like restaking or intent-based architecture. You will not only have traded through these epochs—you will have recorded them. This is the difference between being a tourist and being a chronicler.

Some advanced investors take this further by tagging journal entries by theme: e.g., "Overconfidence," "Narrative-Driven Entry," "Missed Exit Plan." This creates a taxonomy of behaviour that you can analyse periodically. Others rate each decision 1–5 in hindsight, and annotate the rating with what they missed. These systems transform the journal into a dynamic feedback interface—less a diary, more a behavioural analytics engine.

One might argue this is overkill for a "retail investor." But that misses the point. *The very fact that most don't do this is what creates the edge.* In an industry obsessed with alpha, this is internal alpha. It's what allows you to sharpen your mental models while others repeat theirs unconsciously. It's the tool that turns volatility into tuition, rather than trauma.

The habit also scales. If you're managing a fund, building a DAO treasury, or running due diligence for a team, the journaling framework becomes a collaborative resource. Team-wide decision logs align strategy, reduce blame games, and clarify institutional memory. It becomes harder to drift when your thought process is recorded, visible, and subject to review.

Yet perhaps the most underrated benefit is emotional. Crypto investing can feel isolating—especially when markets are down, narratives turn toxic, and attention evaporates. The journal provides continuity. It reminds you that progress is not linear, that past chaos was navigated, that lessons compound. It anchors you when signals are few and noise is deafening.

To build wealth sustainably in this space, you must become a better thinker faster than the market can confuse you. Tools won't do that. Communities won't do that. Only *reflection, structured, consistent, and honest*, can do that. The crypto journal is not a side project—it is the base layer of your intellectual infrastructure.

Writing sharpens memory. Memory clarifies judgement. Judgement compounds value. That's not poetry. That's process.

Chapter 9
The Ethics of Decentralised Wealth

The decentralised financial sphere arrives without a built-in moral compass. That absence is not an oversight; it is a deliberate echo of its philosophical roots. Yet it also functions as a mirror—one in which we are compelled to examine not just our tactics, but our convictions. Now that crypto has shifted from the margins to a recognised part of the world's economic machinery, the question is no longer whether it will scale. It has. The harder question is what ethics, if any, will scale alongside it—or whether the race for profit will simply outrun principle altogether.

Traditional finance, for all its flaws, is steeped in the sediment of centuries: accumulated norms, legal frameworks, institutional oversight. DeFi, by contrast, thrives on permissionlessness. No application forms, no gatekeepers, no central arbitrators. This is liberation for the excluded and fertile ground for the ambitious. Yet it leaves a vacuum. In such a space, decisions are driven not by law or consensus but by sheer ability. The essential moral dilemma of Web3 can be stated plainly: when nothing stands in your way, what does?

Crypto has been hailed, often with evangelical fervour, as a creed of monetary liberation. It promises sovereignty, privacy, control. But sovereignty is not virtue. Control is not conscience. Autonomy without accountability is simply opportunism in disguise. The rise of decentralised wealth—from yield farming and liquid staking to the frothy churn of NFTs and meme coins—has created extraordinary gains. It has also nurtured a culture of financial tinkering that seldom pauses to ask: at whose cost? In this terrain, the line between invention and exploitation can be as thin as a sheet of paper.

Here, those tensions are not swept aside. Nor are they romanticised. Instead, the ethics of decentralised wealth are treated as a living, unresolved inquiry—one that every participant answers not in words, but through choices. Consider the moral greys: front-running bots, MEV (miner extractable value), exploiting flawed smart contracts. Perfectly legal, often profitable, occasionally admired for their technical finesse—yet are they fair? If there is no judge, does that absolve the act? Or does it make personal responsibility all the more acute?

Greed in a permissionless arena is not greed as we once knew it. It wears pseudonyms, runs on automation, and cloaks itself in ideological justifications. "Code is law," some say—as though the possibility of action were its own moral licence. But just as the presence of a lock does not ennoble the lock-picker, the existence of an exploit does not dignify its use. Ethics here is not a restraint on freedom—it is the architecture that makes freedom coherent. Without it, decentralisation risks devolving into a playground for predation rather than a platform for equitable empowerment.

The question "Can crypto be moral?" is not an academic side note—it strikes at the core of legitimacy. If governance is spread across the many, who decides what is right? If a DAO votes through a harmful measure, is that democracy—or mob rule dressed up in smart contracts? If a token surges through coordinated hype, is that community spirit or orchestrated manipulation? The old order assigned ethics to regulators and institutions. The new one deposits them in the crowd's hands. But history offers a blunt reminder: wisdom does not always follow the majority.

The aim here is not to hand down universal laws, but to sketch a framework for ethical self-governance. It asks each actor to define their own lines—not through platitudes, but by interrogating their role, their impact, and the longer story they are contributing to. The argument is not for sameness in conduct, but against thoughtlessness. In decentralised systems, morality is not an external code; it is an internal discipline.

The discussion on *Practising Ethical Capitalism* grounds these ideas in action. It looks at what it means to earn yield without creating collateral harm; to join DAOs that advance fairness as well as token value; to support protocols that value resilience above transient hype. Here, personal integrity is not abstract—it threads directly into protocol design, into the legitimacy of wealth itself. Ethics, far from being a drag on performance, emerge as a pillar of sustainability.

Examples abound. Protocols that reward patience through long-term vesting and participatory governance. NFT projects that reinvest in their communities and commit to open-source tools. Layer-1 chains that build ethical incentives into validator rewards. These are not utopian sketches; they already exist, proving that ethical architecture can take root in Web3.

Still, it would be naïve to assume intent alone will clean the slate. The dilemmas remain: Should one engage with a protocol that is lucrative yet socially questionable? Back a technically brilliant team with opaque governance? Profit from tokens fuelled by hype that lures in the ill-informed? Such questions are not thought experiments—they are weekly realities for serious builders and investors.

No one is expected to resolve them once and for all. Instead, the call is to develop a personal ethos—a compass that draws its bearing not from slogans or crowd sentiment, but from persistent self-interrogation. In decentralised realms, values are not handed down; they are made. And remade. The process is less a proclamation than a habit of alignment, revisited as the tools, protocols, and ambitions evolve.

There is also a generational weight to this. Crypto is not just a market—it is an emerging civic fabric. The behaviours we normalise now will calcify into the norms of tomorrow. Treat yield farming like looting, meme pumps like collective mania, and governance like stagecraft, and you are not merely trading recklessly—you are setting the syllabus for those who follow. Every act here is a lesson. The question is: what lesson will it teach?

Ethics in crypto are not an afterthought to be bolted on after success. They are the very foundation of legitimacy, scalability, and endurance. A project that burns through trust may enjoy a brief ascendancy, but trust, in decentralised networks, is the gravity that keeps everything in orbit. The argument could not be more direct: ethical clarity is not a limitation but a strategic advantage. The next wave of decentralised wealth will not be driven solely by code or clever tokenomics—it will be anchored in principled design and deliberate participation.

Wealth, if we are honest, is not just the stockpiling of assets. It is the capacity to act without the weight of regret. And in decentralised systems, that capacity is not granted—it is earned, patiently, by those willing to build it. This is the invitation, and the challenge.

The Shadow Side of Freedom:

In a world increasingly shaped by surveillance, overreach, and algorithmic governance, the appeal of anonymity and permissionlessness is visceral. Crypto, at its ideological core, emerged not merely as a financial technology but as a philosophical rebellion. It offers exit rather than protest, privacy rather than exposure, and sovereignty rather than submission. These features are not cosmetic—they are foundational. They grant individuals extraordinary autonomy: to move capital, to establish identities, to participate in markets without clearance or credentials. But embedded in this promise is a paradox that decentralised systems have yet to fully confront: *when no one watches, who is responsible?* Freedom, as it turns out, is only as generative as the structures—and the ethics—that support its use.

Anonymity has historically been a shield for the vulnerable. In regimes that persecute dissent, in economies that marginalise the unbanked, and in digital spaces where identity can become a liability, the ability to transact or speak without exposure is not just protective—it is vital. But anonymity also disinhibits. Without the friction of reputation or the cost of social accountability, individuals behave differently. The same cryptographic shield that protects a whistle-blower also enables a rug-pull artist. The smart contract that liberates capital flows from bureaucratic constraint can also be wielded to automate financial harm at scale. This is the shadow side of freedom: the cost of systems that refuse to discriminate is that they cannot distinguish between integrity and exploitation.

Permissionless systems, by design, embrace openness over control. They are meant to be neutral substrates—available to all, coercive to none. But neutrality, while elegant in theory, is not apolitical in practice. When platforms allow any actor to operate—regardless of history, intent, or behaviour—the burden of discernment shifts from system to individual. And most individuals are unequipped, unwilling, or uninterested in vetting every address, evaluating every protocol, or questioning every narrative. In such environments, actors who are willing to operate without conscience often outperform those constrained by it.

Consider the persistence of pump-and-dump schemes, Ponzi protocols, or NFT projects launched with no roadmap beyond hype and exit liquidity. These are not accidental by-products. They are *structurally incentivised behaviours* in environments where transparency exists without consequence and where participants mistake pseudonymity for immunity. In the absence of enforced norms, it is the most normless actors who tend to move fastest and extract most. And yet, these behaviours do not exist in a vacuum—they reshape the culture, signal what is rewarded, and erode the very trust upon which decentralised systems depend.

The argument here is not to impose centralised control onto decentralised systems—that would be a category error. Rather, it is to acknowledge that technological neutrality does not absolve ethical responsibility. Builders, investors, and participants alike must contend with the moral dynamics their tools create. Not just how they *can* be used, but how they *tend* to be used—and whether those tendencies advance the kind of world they claim to want.

Anonymity also introduces a second-order problem: *dislocation from consequence.* In traditional social systems, reputation is an implicit form of currency. It governs behaviour, incentivises reliability, and punishes misconduct through exclusion or sanction. In crypto ecosystems, especially those structured around anonymous or pseudonymous participation, this social layer is often absent or too easily manipulated. Wallet addresses, ENS names, Discord handles—these may carry track records, but they are also disposable. Burn an identity? Simply switch chains, spin up a new pseudonym, and re-enter the system unencumbered. This mechanic, while innovative for privacy, also makes *ethical reincarnation trivial.* And when the cost of starting over is near zero, so too is the deterrent against misbehaviour.

To understand the full implications of this dynamic, it is worth looking beyond crypto. In psychology, the phenomenon known as the "online disinhibition effect" describes how people behave more aggressively, dishonestly, or impulsively in anonymous online settings. The same principle manifests in decentralised finance, only amplified by financial instruments, complex incentives, and liquidity that never sleeps. When people believe they will never be identified, and when systems offer no embedded feedback loop for ethical evaluation, even well-intentioned actors can drift into moral grey zones with surprising ease. *The issue is not malevolence, but ambient detachment.* And detachment is dangerous when paired with leverage and code.

Yet, to reject anonymity outright is to miss its value. It is a vital tool in the architecture of resistance, expression, and experimentation. What's needed is not the elimination of anonymity, but the cultivation of *anonymity with responsibility*. That is, systems and cultures that reward trust-building, even in pseudonymous environments. Protocols that elevate consistent contributors, design mechanisms for accountability, and prioritise *reputation without identity*. This is not a contradiction—it is an emerging design frontier. Proof-of-humanity, on-chain reputation systems, soulbound tokens, and quadratic voting all gesture towards models that preserve freedom while nurturing social trust.

More than any single protocol or product, this tension between empowerment and ethical opacity defines the future of decentralised systems. Freedom must be defended—but not deified. If decentralisation is to be more than a technical achievement, it must mature into a philosophical stance that accepts the full spectrum of its consequences. That includes reckoning with the ways in which freedom—untethered from ethical architecture—can devolve into chaos, opportunism, or harm masked as innovation.

A central thesis of this chapter is that *freedom without friction is rarely generative*. Healthy systems do not eliminate constraint; they *channel it* towards productive outcomes. Traditional systems used gatekeepers, regulations, and institutions to achieve this. Decentralised systems must discover their own analogues—not through force, but through alignment, design, and shared standards. Open participation need not imply open predation. Permissionlessness should not excuse predatory arbitrage. And anonymity should not mean *amnesia* for ethical accountability.

To avoid the pitfalls of permissionless entropy, communities must begin embedding *values into code.* That might mean curating protocol behaviour through governance; penalising extractionist patterns with slashing or social staking; rewarding behaviour that benefits the network rather than cannibalises it. It might also mean changing the culture: celebrating long-term thinking over fast exits, transparency over mystique, stewardship over spectacle. These are not aesthetic choices—they are existential decisions about what decentralised wealth will mean and what kind of society it will build.

Freedom is fragile. It requires vigilance, not just from regulators, but from every participant. The shadow side of decentralisation is not merely a technical challenge—it is a philosophical one. And it will not be solved with better code alone. It demands a generation of users who view freedom not as a licence, but as a responsibility—who understand that in a world where no one is watching, *how you act defines who you are.* This is the ethical frontier of Web3. It is not about limiting freedom, but *elevating it.*

Greed in a Permissionless World:

There is no firewall between ambition and exploitation in a permissionless system. That is both its greatest strength and its deepest vulnerability. When participation is unrestricted and code becomes law, it creates not just a playground for innovation—but a testing ground for ethics. Nowhere is this more evident than in the question of *greed.* In the decentralised world of crypto markets, the old lines between cleverness and cunning, profit and predation, opportunism and exploitation become blurred. This is not simply a financial puzzle. It is a moral one. And increasingly, it is a defining challenge for the credibility of the crypto ecosystem.

At first glance, decentralised finance appears meritocratic: the barriers are low, the rules are transparent, and outcomes are dictated by algorithmic consensus. But strip away the technical architecture and what remains is an evolving moral theatre where individuals are incentivised to test limits, exploit edge cases, and pursue asymmetric advantages that traditional systems would either outlaw or moderate. It is this *edge-hunting behaviour*—from sniping NFT mints to arbitraging broken tokenomics—that poses the essential question: when everything is allowed, what is right?

The answer depends less on law and more on *self-regulation.* That, in turn, depends on a shared sense of legitimacy. Yet, crypto's cultural legitimacy remains fragile—partly because its financial legitimacy is frequently undermined by bad actors extracting value through morally ambiguous means. Consider the practice of "MEV" (Maximal Extractable Value), where sophisticated bots reorder blockchain transactions to front-run or sandwich other users. Technically legal. Practically invisible. Ethically corrosive. It is a clear instance where strategy has outpaced scrutiny, and where decentralisation's openness becomes a vector for silent abuse.

These are not niche concerns. When economic rewards are uncoupled from productive contribution—when money flows not to those who build, but to those who exploit—the long-term consequences are systemic. Trust erodes. Reputation decays. Networks hollow out. A decentralised future becomes difficult to defend when its visible fruits are dominated by scams, exit liquidity, and rug pulls. More dangerously, when these practices are normalised or glamorised—as "just how the game is played"—it sends a signal that participation is a matter of cunning, not contribution. *And when cunning rules, legitimacy is impossible to scale.*

To be clear: the profit motive itself is not the issue. Crypto does not need to be ascetic to be ethical. But systems that reward extraction over value creation become unsustainable. Greed, unchecked, becomes a systemic attack vector. When too many actors prioritise short-term gain over long-term alignment, the network loses its gravity. Community splinters. Incentives fracture. The protocol's economics may survive, but its *ethics collapse silently.* This collapse often escapes attention—until it no longer can.

Contrast this with traditional markets, where regulation acts as a proxy for morality. Insider trading, pump-and-dump schemes, or fraudulent disclosures are policed not simply because they are harmful, but because they violate a shared economic contract between market and public. Crypto, by removing many of these regulatory layers, removes that proxy. What replaces it—at least in theory—is open-source transparency and decentralised consensus. But *transparency is not morality*, and consensus is not conscience. If anything, the speed and fluidity of blockchain transactions mean that bad behaviour can be replicated, amplified, and forgotten in record time.

Moreover, crypto operates in a cross-jurisdictional vacuum. What is legal in one country may be illegal in another. What is frowned upon in traditional finance may be normalised in Web3. This liminality—the "grey zone" between law and ethics—is where many of the most profitable opportunities lie. Think of early liquidity providers in protocols designed to fail, or influencers paid under the table to shill tokens they quietly dump on followers. Again, none of these acts are necessarily illegal. But legality is not the same as *legitimacy*. The market might not penalise these behaviours, but the culture does. Over time, credibility becomes a harder currency than coin.

Some argue this is simply the Darwinism of free markets. That systems without gatekeepers will always attract both pioneers and predators. That the role of the user is not to moralise but to adapt. But this techno-pragmatism is a dangerous abdication of responsibility. In systems where code is law, the values embedded in that code *are governance*. And when that governance favours velocity over accountability, speculation over stewardship, or anonymity over responsibility, it produces a system optimised for *self-serving cleverness rather than shared prosperity*.

We must also reckon with the fact that decentralised systems flatten moral nuance. A DAO smart contract cannot tell the difference between an honest yield farmer and a mercenary whale. A DEX cannot distinguish between liquidity provision and manipulation. And when these systems treat all actions as equal—so long as they are technically valid—they flatten the ethical register of the entire ecosystem. *The result is not neutrality. It is moral numbness.*

That numbness is compounded by the social architecture of crypto itself. Discord servers move at speed. Twitter narratives dominate discourse. Thoughtful analysis is often drowned by meme cycles, hype trains, and virtue signalling. Within this attention economy, the line between ethical success and opportunistic success is further blurred. Those who criticise extractive behaviours are often accused of gatekeeping; those who exploit them are framed as "early" or "smart." The result is a collective gaslighting where being ethical becomes an *optional aesthetic* rather than a structural commitment.

Yet, there is a growing undercurrent of resistance to this cynicism. Increasingly, founders are embedding ethical commitments into tokenomics. Protocols are experimenting with guardrails: vesting schedules, decentralised governance with reputation systems, and community-elected multisigs. Builders are proposing forms of *conscious capitalism*, where financial incentives are aligned not just to reward but to *retain integrity*. Importantly, these are not post-hoc corrections. They are signs of a maturing ecosystem attempting to *institutionalise values without centralisation.*

The core challenge is cultural, not technical. It is about creating systems where ethics are not enforced by authority, but reinforced by architecture. Where the invisible hand of the market is counterbalanced by the visible will of a value-driven community. Where the most lucrative play is not the one that exploits grey zones, but the one that sustains the commons. This is not idealism—it is strategy. Because in the long run, *only networks that people trust will endure.*

A final tension worth examining is between permissionlessness and accountability. Crypto enthusiasts often celebrate the former while ignoring the latter. But if anyone can build anything, then everyone is responsible for what gets built. If anyone can participate, then everyone must decide *how*. And if value can flow frictionlessly, then judgement must flow with it. Greed, in this context, is not just an individual impulse—it is a test of collective values. What do we reward? What do we overlook? What do we justify?

The decentralised future will not be judged solely by its technological achievements, but by the *character of its incentives*. It will be shaped not by how much wealth it creates, but by *how* that wealth is pursued. The grey zones of permissionless systems are not anomalies—they are where the soul of the system is revealed. And it is there, in that ambiguity, that the future of crypto will be decided. Not just as an asset class, but as a civilisation layer.

Can Crypto Be Moral?

If morality requires accountability, what happens when systems are designed to remove it? This is the essential philosophical question posed by decentralised technologies. When a blockchain network replaces institutions with protocols, when tokens replace titles and smart contracts replace trust, we are no longer just engineering finance—we are reprogramming the ethics of participation. The central dilemma is stark: if no one controls the system, who defines what is right?

Crypto's foundational ethos—permissionlessness—is often framed as a liberatory ideal. Anyone can build, anyone can transact, and anyone can innovate without needing institutional approval. But this freedom, while catalytic for creativity, also erodes traditional moral guardrails. In decentralised environments, power is flattened and fragmented. There is no CEO, no regulator, no singular moral authority. Instead, agency is distributed across nodes, wallets, DAOs, and protocols. This raises a confronting truth: *without a clear locus of control, morality becomes a moving target—negotiated rather than enforced.*

This decentralised moral terrain invites both promise and peril. On one hand, it offers the possibility of self-governing systems that transcend geographic and political constraints—where users shape their own destinies and communities define their own norms. On the other, it opens the door to relativism, opportunism, and collective indifference. Without centralised oversight, actors are incentivised to push the limits of technical possibility, not necessarily ethical responsibility. What is permitted by the code becomes synonymous with what is acceptable. Yet *legalism is not ethics, and technical validity is not moral legitimacy.*

Consider the rise of decentralised autonomous organisations (DAOs). In theory, DAOs are embodiments of democratic governance—crypto-native communities that vote on their own rules, funding priorities, and cultural norms. But in practice, many DAOs are plagued by voter apathy, whale dominance, or governance theatre. When the majority is silent and the minority is strategic, decisions may be procedurally fair but morally hollow. Who speaks for the marginalised in a DAO? Who ensures that power is not simply redistributed but reimagined? The mere presence of a voting mechanism does not guarantee a moral compass. *Decentralisation does not automatically mean justice—it simply removes gatekeepers.*

The ethics of crypto are also strained by the structure of its incentives. Early adoption is often rewarded disproportionately. First movers benefit not just from innovation but from network effects and token inflation. This has created a culture where being early is often more lucrative than being right, and where timing trumps contribution. It's a dynamic that can resemble a pyramid more than a platform. When value accrues to the few at the top while risks cascade to the many at the bottom, we must ask: *is this still an ethical system, or simply an efficient one?*

Take, for example, the case of algorithmic stablecoins. Designed to maintain peg through code-based market incentives, many of these systems promise decentralised stability—yet collapse catastrophically when assumptions fail. Terra's UST is a case in point. When it unravelled, billions in investor value were destroyed, affecting not just speculative traders but ordinary users who trusted the system's perceived reliability. There were no regulators to appeal to, no insurance funds to draw from, no oversight to question faulty design. The result was financial loss, reputational damage, and a public trust deficit. In this context, *the absence of accountability is not neutrality—it is negligence.*

Morality in crypto is also challenged by its anonymity features. Privacy-preserving tools like mixers and zero-knowledge proofs have legitimate use cases—protecting dissidents, shielding vulnerable populations, and enabling financial autonomy. But they are also used to obfuscate illicit gains, launder money, and avoid scrutiny. This duality presents a classic ethical tension: *can a tool be neutral if its most frequent use undermines the public good?* Privacy is a right—but like all rights, it carries responsibilities. When anonymity enables impunity, the line between protection and evasion becomes dangerously thin.

Some defenders of crypto argue that morality is emergent, not imposed—that values will evolve organically as communities mature. There is merit to this view. Open-source culture encourages iterative learning, and crypto-native builders are increasingly experimenting with norms of transparency, inclusion, and long-termism. Platforms like Gitcoin have championed public goods funding. Regenerative finance (ReFi) projects seek to embed environmental and social goals into tokenomics. These are early but important signals that *ethics can be endogenous to the system*—not just imported from traditional finance.

However, emergent ethics are not always sufficient. Relying on communities to self-correct assumes that incentives and values are naturally aligned. But as history has shown—from the 2008 financial crisis to the excesses of Web2—systems rarely self-regulate effectively at scale. What is needed is *intentional design*: architectures that embed moral constraints into the infrastructure itself. This could mean smart contracts that include impact weighting. Protocols that penalise extractive behaviours. Governance frameworks that mandate social audits alongside financial ones. The moral dimension of code must be deliberate, not incidental.

Another key dilemma lies in crypto's relationship with global inequality. Decentralisation is often touted as a leveller—a way for individuals in unstable economies to access global markets, build wealth, and escape monetary repression. There are indeed powerful examples of crypto enabling remittances, micro-finance, and censorship resistance. But the same tools can exacerbate inequality when access, literacy, and capital are unevenly distributed. Yield farming, for example, often favours those with the most capital and the best information. If the architecture privileges insiders, then decentralisation becomes a rhetorical fig leaf—not a transformative ideal.

So, can crypto be moral? The honest answer is: *only if we make it so.* Morality in decentralised systems cannot be outsourced—it must be internalised. It must be practised not just in code, but in culture. Not just in product, but in purpose. That means builders asking not only "can we?" but "should we?" It means communities holding each other accountable, not through outrage cycles, but through principled engagement. It means designing for longevity, not just velocity.

Ultimately, the question is not whether crypto can be moral, but whether we can build systems that *demand morality even when no one is watching*. This is the challenge of trustless infrastructure: it removes the need to trust the system, but it does not remove the need to *be trustworthy within it*. In a world of permissionless participation, values are not enforced—they are *embodied*. The future of decentralised finance will not be defined by technological progress alone, but by the *ethical imagination of those who build it*.

Crypto is not exempt from morality. If anything, it is *more exposed to it*. Every block recorded on-chain is a record not just of data, but of decisions—decisions that shape economies, societies, and lives. In that sense, decentralised systems are mirrors. They reflect our priorities, our assumptions, our blind spots. Whether those reflections produce a better world depends not on the technology, but on *us*.

Practicing Ethical Capitalism:

The mythology of crypto is often steeped in disruption—breaking monopolies, bypassing banks, and reimagining the internet's economic layer. But once the dust of innovation settles, a quieter question emerges: not *what* will we build, but *why*? Practising ethical capitalism within decentralised finance is not a matter of public relations or branding—it is the philosophical spine of long-term relevance. If we accept that code is law, then it follows that capital is legislation. Where it flows, who it empowers, and how it is governed are all reflections of the values we inscribe into economic design. In this context, redefining wealth from mere accumulation to measurable impact is not idealistic—it's a necessity for legitimacy.

Crypto presents a rare opportunity to reassess capitalism from the first principles up. Traditional financial systems—layered with intermediaries, skewed incentives, and opaque governance—have distanced wealth creation from ethical scrutiny. Outcomes are rewarded over processes; scale over intention. The result is a system where maximising shareholder return has often trumped societal well-being. Crypto, by contrast, offers programmable money and programmable governance. *If designed with intention, it can reconnect profit with principle—aligning market incentives with public good.* The tools exist. What's missing is widespread moral fluency.

Practising ethical capitalism in crypto begins with how we define success. Conventional finance glorifies speed, volume, and volatility. Crypto culture has too often mirrored this—celebrating rapid token gains, meme-driven pumps, and short-term arbitrage. Yet the most durable projects in this space increasingly reflect a different philosophy: *slow capital, strong community, sustainable alignment.* Protocols that resist extractive behaviour and reward contribution over speculation are not just more ethical—they are more antifragile. They survive downturns, attract purpose-driven builders, and cultivate long-term user trust.

Consider the model of quadratic funding as pioneered by Gitcoin. Unlike traditional grant structures, quadratic funding allocates capital not based on donor size alone, but on the *number* of donors supporting a project. The result is a system that amplifies community voice and deprioritises elite capture. It's a structural intervention—a financial mechanic embedded with democratic values. Ethical capitalism in crypto is not a slogan; it's *an architecture.* The way a DAO structures its treasury, the tokenomics of a yield protocol, the governance dynamics of an NFT community—all of these are moral decisions in economic clothing.

The ethical investor in crypto must therefore operate with two lenses: the micro (what am I participating in?) and the macro (what kind of system am I reinforcing?). Investing in a high-yield protocol without understanding how those yields are generated may bring temporary gains—but it also perpetuates opacity. Participating in a DAO without engaging in governance may seem harmless—but it slowly corrodes the legitimacy of decentralised participation. *Every wallet signature is an endorsement. Every capital allocation is a moral statement.* This is the burden—and privilege—of decentralised capitalism.

One practical way to approach ethical decision-making in crypto is through the framework of externalities. A project may offer impressive returns, but at what cost to others? Does it depend on constant new user inflow (Ponzi dynamics)? Does it externalise risk to unsophisticated retail participants? Does it compromise long-term protocol health for short-term liquidity spikes? Ethical analysis demands that we look beyond token price and examine *systemic impact*. Just as ESG frameworks attempt to evaluate environmental, social, and governance factors in traditional finance, crypto must develop its own analytical tools—not watered-down moral checklists, but rigorous, crypto-native metrics of ethical value creation.

This also requires us to reckon with distribution. A decentralised protocol in name only—one where insiders hold 80% of the token supply and governance is captured by a handful of actors—is not truly decentralised. Equity matters. Not simply in token distribution, but in access to participation, education, and upside. Ethical capitalism is not about perfect equality, but about *fair asymmetry*—where those who contribute meaningfully are rewarded meaningfully, and where systems are designed to be legible, inclusive, and resilient.

Yet ethical capitalism also involves restraint. In a space obsessed with growth, the refusal to exploit grey zones is itself a radical act. Avoiding regulatory arbitrage when it's easy. Choosing not to list a token that lacks fundamentals, even if it could drive fees. Deliberately capping returns to prioritise long-term health over short-term hype. These decisions are rarely rewarded in the short term—but they build reputational compounding, a currency of trust far more durable than any token.

We must also reframe wealth not as possession, but as *stewardship*. In crypto, where gains can be asymmetric and sudden, the moral challenge is not just how we earn, but how we distribute, contribute, and share. Treasury diversification, community grants, retroactive public goods funding—these are not philanthropic add-ons. They are *core components* of regenerative economies. The most admired leaders in crypto today are those who give transparently, fund openly, and design with post-personal incentives in mind. They understand that *capital is not the endgame, but the amplifier of values.*

Of course, ethical capitalism is not without friction. It requires trade-offs. Slower launches. Higher standards. Lower short-term returns. But it also invites deeper engagement, richer communities, and more aligned ecosystems. The projects that endure—like Ethereum, Yearn, or Optimism—are those that have internalised the discipline of ethics not as constraint, but as *compass.* They understand that impact compounds. That reputation is a moat. That ethics is the ultimate form of scaling trust.

And trust is the foundational currency of decentralisation. Without it, all we have is code—mechanical, indifferent, manipulable. With it, we have systems that scale coordination, honour contributions, and embed meaning into money. *Ethical capitalism in crypto is not about moral purity. It's about conscious design.* The willingness to think long, act justly, and build structures that outlast personalities.

Redefining wealth as impact requires a re-education of ambition. It invites us to shift from acquisition to contribution, from speculation to stewardship, from extraction to regeneration. This is not only a philosophical pivot. It's a practical one. The next wave of builders and investors will not win by moving faster—they will win by *building deeper.* Ethics is not a constraint on innovation. It is its *greatest differentiator.* The question is no longer whether we can build wealth with crypto. It is whether that wealth will *mean* something.

Because wealth that doesn't serve people, uplift communities, or steward futures is not wealth. It is accumulation. And *accumulation without purpose is erosion in disguise.*

Chapter 10
Inner Wealth – What You Keep When the Charts Collapse

Being able to watch one's net worth tick up or down in real time has not made us feel richer. If anything, it has sharpened the edge of our anxiety. In a world of markets that never sleep, dashboards that refresh by the second, and bots that trade without blinking, crypto does more than test our grasp of finance—it probes our capacity for inner steadiness. As the violent swings of digital assets blur the line between disciplined investing and compulsive monitoring, a quieter question emerges: what remains when the charts turn south? When the wallet balance stalls, when the thrill of gains evaporates, when an identity built on winning must sit with stillness? This is a chapter about what endures beyond wealth—not measured in currency, but in depth.

Inner wealth is no rival to financial achievement. Rather, it's what lends that achievement weight, coherence, and dignity. Yet in the sprawling architecture of decentralised finance, it is conspicuously absent. You won't see it in most whitepapers. It's rarely coded into tokenomics. Few community forums give it a name. And without it, even the most lavish portfolio risks becoming an echo chamber for fear, greed, and endless speculation. To conquer the market without also mastering the mind is not progress—it's a sleek, digitised form of self-delusion. The real work of crypto extends beyond staking rewards and liquidity pools; it demands an internal reckoning. How does one inhabit abundance without being hollowed by it? How does one weather volatility without outsourcing emotional stability to the shifting lines of a price chart?

The first doorway is gratitude—stripped of cliché, treated as a disciplined awareness rather than a decorative sentiment. Digital wealth is rarely earned by effort alone; it's shaped by timing, access, and a measure of fortune. The capacity to deploy capital into an emerging protocol, to self-custody assets, to read a smart contract's logic—these are digital privileges, denied to billions. This realisation should not breed guilt, but perspective. Private keys are not just strings of data; they are keys to freedoms others do not hold. Recognising that changes the flavour of every gain. It prompts the question: what will I do with this advantage? Will I steward it with care, or fritter it away in the endless race of comparison?

And comparison is crypto's quiet undertow. Every transaction is public, every wallet traceable. Leaderboards, alpha leaks, and victory laps on social feeds—all engineered to provoke reaction, not reflection. It's here that the scarcity mindset seeps in, almost unnoticed. The question mutates from "Am I wealthy?" to "Am I wealthier than the one who caught that presale last week?" In that shift, enoughness becomes a mirage. The problem is not technological—it's narrative. So long as sufficiency is borrowed from external markers, we remain at the mercy of systems we claim to transcend.

What's needed is a reset—not the rejection of ambition, but a recalibration of its aim. Are we optimising for visibility on a scoreboard, or for sovereignty over our time, choices, and mind? Are we stacking tokens to impress the unseen, or to gain the freedom to live, work, and give on our own terms? The pivot comes when success is measured not in sheer accumulation, but in contribution. Not "How much is mine?" but "What does this make possible, and who else benefits?" This isn't moral window-dressing—it's strategic. Investors anchored in values tend to trade less, react less, and construct systems that defend their long game instead of eroding it.

At the heart of this is the notion of a post-wealth life. It's a confronting question: if money ceased to be a concern tomorrow, what would you do? Many discover their answer is foggy, revealing that money has shifted from means to mask—a way to defer the deeper work of naming purpose. Inner wealth begins when that mask is dropped. When capital is reclassified as a tool: to shape time with intent, to bring presence to relationships, to channel effort into creation, service, or mastery. These are not ornamental ideals. They are anchors in a sea designed to distract.

The paradox is that crypto's abstractions—wallet addresses, token IDs, automated protocols—can push aside the most human questions: What do I value? What is a good life? The technology offers speed, reach, anonymity. It cannot offer direction. That choice is ours alone. Inner wealth fixes the compass, stopping capital from spinning us outwards into fragmentation. And it is not a prize to be claimed after fortune is made—it must grow alongside it. Every swap, every governance vote, every decision to hold or sell is a mirror as much as a trade.

The urgency here lies not merely in market volatility, but in the youth of the crypto space itself—fast, loud, and largely unexamined. There is little generational wisdom to inherit, few elders to lean on. Most navigate it alone, learning through abrupt wins and sharper losses, in an environment that rewards the loud and confident more than the reflective. But as the capital inflow grows, so too does the psychic bill for unexamined behaviour: burnout, compulsive patterns, isolation. These are not fringe anomalies—they are common. And they will not be solved by a more aggressive yield strategy. They are addressed only by building a clearer, sturdier inner framework.

In the pages ahead, we'll explore that framework—not with fluffy affirmations, but with tangible practices: philosophical reframing, gratitude as mental training, mapping values into action, casting forward into your post-wealth self. The aim is not simply to inspire but to clarify, so that what matters is visible before the market forces the lesson. Because for wealth to mean more than numbers, it must be readable, ownable, and stitched to personal significance.

You will be asked to inspect the machinery under your ambition. Is it driven by legacy, security, creativity—or the quieter fear of missing out? You will be invited to separate financial freedom from emotional freedom. To question the cult of optimisation. To ask what "more" is really meant to fix. And to envision a life plotted not on volatility's curve, but on volition's map—where your calendar mirrors your values, your energy is your most guarded asset, and your gains sharpen clarity rather than blur it.

This is not a choice between wealth and wisdom. It is an understanding that wealth becomes whole only when wisdom sits at its centre. Without inner wealth, even the most cunning crypto strategy is just leverage without leadership. With it, every asset becomes secondary to agency; every windfall is refracted through the lens of enough; every market collapse loses its sting, because your worth was never tied to the jagged line on the chart—it was in how you lived while it moved.

Consider this chapter a compass, not a map. It won't dictate your route, but it will press the questions that determine whether the destination, when reached, is worth the journey. This is the terrain of crypto that isn't obsessed with the next explosive rally, but with what remains when the market is emptied out and the mirror is the only thing looking back. Inner wealth—what survives the cycle. Let's begin there.

Detachment as a Financial Skill:

The most overlooked form of financial intelligence is not predictive modelling, high-frequency trading, or early access to token allocations—it is detachment. Not apathy, nor indifference, but the cultivated ability to hold wealth without being held by it. In a system where liquidity never sleeps and market sentiment can swing from euphoria to despair within a single tweet, detachment becomes not just a virtue, but a strategic edge. *The emotionally reactive investor is always at the mercy of others' volatility. The detached investor is governed by internal clarity, not external chaos.*

Detachment in this context does not mean disengagement. It means *non-identification.* You may own assets without conflating them with your self-worth. You may play the game of capital allocation without letting the scoreboard dictate your sense of peace. And most importantly, you can remain agile—mentally and strategically—because you are not clinging to a particular outcome or narrative. *This is not detachment from responsibility, but detachment from illusion.* Illusions such as: that wealth guarantees meaning; that losses define failure; that volatility is a verdict on your intelligence. These ideas, left unexamined, corrode both your emotional stability and your decision-making.

One of the most insidious risks in crypto is not financial loss—it is identity enmeshment. When a rising wallet balance becomes your proxy for competence, foresight, or superiority, detachment dissolves. So does learning. Because now, every market correction feels like an existential referendum. This psychological fragility often masquerades as conviction—until the tide turns. True detachment is what allows an individual to learn from mistakes, not deny them. To accept being wrong without being wounded. To change thesis without shame. Detachment, paradoxically, enhances both humility and rigour.

Consider the design of most crypto platforms: dopamine-rich, signal-saturated, and deeply gamified. Interfaces are engineered to provoke compulsive checking. Alerts invite immediate reaction. Real-time PnL tools condition users into associating value with constant motion. This is not neutral UX. It is architecture designed to erode stillness. And if you don't notice it, you become its product. Detachment, in this setting, is a countercultural act. It's what allows you to install boundaries—on screen time, on reaction speed, on portfolio micromanagement. Not because you're lazy, but because you've recognised that *clarity compounds when distraction is minimised.*

The case for detachment becomes even clearer when we study professional investors who outperform consistently over decades. Across disciplines—from Buffett to Dalio to Novogratz—there is one recurring pattern: a strong separation between ego and asset. They do not marry their positions. They do not chase every trend. They do not confuse movement with progress. What they cultivate instead is patience, systems, and perspective. *Detachment is the substrate beneath all three.* It is what allows them to act when others panic, and wait when others scramble. It is a kind of disciplined emotional sobriety in a drunken marketplace.

Of course, critics may argue that detachment risks disinterest—that if you're too removed, you miss opportunities or lack drive. But this misunderstands the nature of strategic detachment. It is not the opposite of passion; it is the container that preserves it. Without detachment, passion becomes obsession. And obsession in markets often leads to poor risk management, tunnel vision, and unsustainable behaviour. The detached mind can still be deeply curious, deeply invested—but not enslaved. It sees more clearly because it's not clouded by over-identification or inflated self-concept.

There is also an ethical dimension to detachment that deserves attention. When your sense of value is overly tethered to your holdings, you're more likely to rationalise harmful decisions: pump-and-dump participation, misinformation, or reckless speculation disguised as conviction. But when identity is unlatched from outcomes, your integrity becomes harder to compromise. You're no longer willing to win at any cost, because the win no longer defines you. *This is where detachment becomes not just personal hygiene, but collective responsibility.* In a decentralised system, character is currency—and detachment keeps that character intact when pressure mounts.

The cultivation of detachment is not a singular act; it's a practice. It begins by observing your own mental patterns: How do I feel when my portfolio rises? When it falls? What do I make those fluctuations mean? Am I more engaged with price than with process? From there, you can begin to install systems that protect your clarity. Journaling decisions rather than checking them compulsively. Using automation to reduce reactive trading. Allocating a portion of capital to "untouchable" long-term positions. Each of these mechanisms is an externalisation of an internal stance: *I am not my portfolio. I am the thinker behind it.*

This mental posture also enables you to engage with long-term wealth more effectively. Detachment expands your time horizon, because you're no longer trying to prove something on a weekly or monthly scale. You can zoom out, study cycles, and make fewer—but better—decisions. *The more loosely you hold the need to be right immediately, the more likely you are to be right eventually.* Investors who master detachment resist the tyranny of short-term performance. They're more likely to understand that *peace is a form of profit.* Not every gain needs to be financial. Sometimes, not trading is the victory.

From a psychological standpoint, detachment is best understood not as suppressing emotion but as *repositioning awareness.* You're still allowed to feel excitement or disappointment—but you no longer allow those emotions to dictate your behaviour. This is especially important in crypto, where emotional contagion spreads at light speed. One person's panic becomes a community's sell-off. One influencer's conviction becomes a narrative flood. Detachment is your circuit breaker. It is what keeps you aligned with principles rather than pressure. And it is what makes you a stabilising force—not just for yourself, but for those around you.

Real-world examples illuminate the power of detachment. During the 2020–2021 bull run, countless investors rode dramatic gains only to lose everything by overtrading the drawdowns. Many had no exit plans, no principles—only emotion and momentum. Others, by contrast, held calmly, rebalanced systematically, and avoided the siren song of leverage. Their portfolios grew more slowly, but endured. And those who weathered that cycle with detachment emerged not just with capital, but with confidence—the kind that can't be shaken by noise, because it was never built on noise.

Detachment also redefines what we think of as wealth. If your peace is fragile, conditional on market conditions, then you are not yet free—regardless of your net worth. If your relationships suffer when your portfolio does, you are not yet sovereign. Inner wealth, as discussed earlier in this book, is not a luxury add-on to financial literacy—it is its foundation. And detachment is its daily expression. Every time you decline to panic, to chase, to compare—you affirm your autonomy. *You demonstrate that the market may move, but you do not have to be moved with it.*

In the broader arc of decentralised finance, where speed, novelty, and complexity often crowd out introspection, detachment offers something rare: space. The space to choose intentionally. The space to evaluate independently. The space to define success on your own terms. It is not about resisting change, but about anchoring within it. Because the markets will always change. Trends will come and go. Narratives will inflate and collapse. But your ability to remain centred—unattached, but not disengaged—is what will determine whether crypto is a source of power or a source of instability in your life.

Ultimately, detachment is not a rejection of ambition, nor a retreat from markets. It is a refusal to allow external volatility to colonise your inner world. It is the practice of separating performance from peace, outcomes from identity. And it is what allows you to show up—again and again—not with desperation, but with discernment.

In a system that rewards quick wins but rarely teaches endurance, *detachment is how you stay intelligent for longer than others can stay reactive.* It is how you stop being manipulated by charts and start being guided by clarity.

That clarity is what this subchapter—and this entire book—has sought to offer: not just tools for external wealth, but frameworks for inner sovereignty. And in this, detachment is not a cold intellectual stance. It is a quiet revolution. One that allows you to hold the future lightly, and move through it wisely.

Gratitude in the Age of Digital Abundance:

We live in a time when a person with a modest internet connection, a smartphone, and a self-custodied wallet can access financial tools that rival the capabilities of an entire institutional infrastructure from just two decades ago. The very idea that an individual can create, transfer, or grow wealth outside the gatekeeping of banks, governments, and geographic borders would have sounded utopian in the early 2000s. Yet today, these capabilities are not only available—they are often taken for granted. In the discourse around crypto, there is endless emphasis on scale, speed, innovation, and profit. But rarely do we pause to acknowledge the quiet privilege embedded in digital access itself. *Gratitude, in this age of digital abundance, is not sentimentality—it is structural awareness.*

To speak of gratitude in the context of decentralised wealth might seem quaint or even off-topic. But it is, in fact, a critical calibration. Without it, the abundance of tools and opportunities risks fostering entitlement rather than clarity. Many enter the crypto space animated by a hunger to "make it"—and that hunger, while understandable, can distort perspective. When every price dip feels like an injustice, when every missed opportunity is framed as betrayal by the market, it is easy to lose touch with the fact that even having access to this ecosystem is itself a rare global privilege. Consider: more than 2.5 billion people still lack reliable internet. Millions more live under regimes where digital expression is censored and financial autonomy is structurally suppressed. The ability to transact peer-to-peer, hold assets in private keys, or even learn from decentralised platforms is not globally guaranteed. It is a geopolitical luxury.

Digital privilege is not a guilt-inducing concept—it is a clarifying one. It reminds us that access to crypto is not merely about being "early" but about being *positioned.* Geography, education, language, regulatory environment, and socioeconomic status all create uneven entry points. When someone in Berlin can deploy capital into a DeFi protocol while someone in Lagos faces infrastructural throttles just to access a stable internet connection, it reframes what "opportunity" means. Recognising this asymmetry invites not just compassion but intention. *Gratitude becomes the bridge between personal gain and collective responsibility.* If we do not cultivate it, the abundance of digital tools risks reinforcing the very hierarchies crypto set out to challenge.

It also shifts how we relate to volatility. Market cycles—especially in crypto—can feel brutal. Values can collapse overnight. Promising projects can implode. Yet amid these collapses, the foundational affordances often remain: you can still self-custody, still transact permissionlessly, still move assets globally in minutes. The infrastructure does not vanish with the price chart. *Gratitude reframes loss.* It doesn't erase disappointment but tempers it with perspective. When your identity is tethered only to market performance, every downturn becomes existential. When it's tethered to deeper awareness—of how much is still possible—losses are absorbed, not exaggerated.

Practically, this mindset shift influences behaviour. Investors rooted in entitlement often chase. They act from scarcity—fearful that if they do not maximise every trade, they're failing. They treat wealth as a sprint. But those grounded in gratitude are more strategic. They act from sufficiency, not desperation. They understand that wealth, like health, compounds best through consistency, not feverish optimisation. This doesn't mean they lack ambition—it means their ambition is stabilised by perspective. They take gains with humility, sit through downturns with patience, and reallocate not with anxiety but with clarity. *Gratitude builds durable conviction, while entitlement feeds burnout.*

There's also a philosophical layer to consider. We are conditioned, particularly in Western market cultures, to define success as expansion. More assets. More yield. More leverage. Crypto amplifies this bias. The culture celebrates exponential returns and generational wealth creation. But rarely does it interrogate what any of this is *for.* What is the endpoint of "making it" if it's not accompanied by meaning? Gratitude invites this interrogation. It asks: if you already have more optionality, mobility, and sovereignty than most humans have ever had, what are you building toward? What responsibility follows from that privilege? The most liberated person in the world—digitally or otherwise—is still impoverished if they lack a sense of enoughness.

This is where gratitude becomes more than just a mindset—it becomes *a system of values.* When you recognise what you already have, you're less likely to exploit, manipulate, or dehumanise in pursuit of more. You're more inclined to use your tools thoughtfully, your influence responsibly, your knowledge generously. Gratitude in a decentralised context becomes a counterweight to the darker impulses that the permissionless environment enables: unchecked speculation, extractive behaviour, toxic tribalism. It acts as an internal regulator where external ones are minimal. *In a permissionless system, ethics must be self-imposed—and gratitude is a gateway to ethics.*

It also reshapes how we teach others. If we model crypto as just a game of financial arbitrage, we pass down a culture of opportunism. But if we model it as access—a chance to engage with wealth-building on unprecedented terms—then we transmit values alongside information. We begin to see education as inheritance, not just content distribution. A crypto wallet given to a child can be more than a financial seed—it can be a vessel for stewardship, intentionality, and purpose. But only if we embed those meanings into it. And gratitude is what does that embedding. It gives symbolic weight to otherwise mechanical actions.

Consider the narrative of "retiring early through crypto." For many, this is framed as an escape from labour. But the deeper promise is not freedom *from* work—it's freedom *for* meaningful work. Gratitude reframes this aspiration. Instead of obsessing over financial exit velocity, it asks: what will I contribute when I no longer have to chase survival? What can I offer when I'm no longer dominated by financial anxiety? These are not abstract questions. They're design prompts. And the answers are only as good as the mindset behind them. *Without gratitude, early financial freedom risks becoming early existential drift.*

In practical terms, cultivating gratitude in the age of digital abundance might look like deliberate rituals: journaling not just portfolio performance, but lessons learned; reflecting weekly on what crypto access has enabled in your life beyond capital; diversifying not just across assets but across purposes—so that not every move is about return, but some are about learning, sharing, or exploring. It also looks like contributing to ecosystems without expecting direct return: open-source development, educational content, or even onboarding a relative into a self-custody framework. These acts are not just moral—they're strategic. They build social capital, reputational trust, and long-term resilience in the ecosystem itself.

It's worth noting that gratitude does not require perfection. You can still want more, still pursue gains, still optimise your strategy. But the quality of your pursuit changes. You're less reactive, more reflective. Less extractive, more expansive. You hold ambition and contentment in the same hand. This is a hard equilibrium to maintain in a culture that fetishises speed. But it is precisely what will distinguish the enduring builders from the temporary speculators. And it will determine whether crypto becomes a sustainable wealth paradigm—or just another gold rush in new clothing.

Ultimately, the practice of gratitude in digital finance is not a moral add-on. It is a foundational lens. It asks: what does it mean to thrive in a system of radical optionality? What becomes possible when we stop seeing access as entitlement and start seeing it as invitation? And how do we build—not just portfolios—but *lives* that honour the magnitude of what this technology makes available?

Gratitude may seem like a soft virtue in a hard-edged industry. But in truth, it is among the most subversive. Because it tells us that we already have enough to build meaning. That the real wealth was never just in the tokens—it was in the tools, the choices, the autonomy they offered. And when we act from that awareness, we stop merely consuming innovation. We start *inhabiting* it. Thoughtfully. Accountably. Gratefully.

Scarcity vs Sufficiency:

Every crypto cycle reveals more than just volatility in prices—it reveals volatility in psychology. Behind every impulsive trade, every frantic tweet, every sleepless night watching candles on a chart, lies a quiet but potent emotion: scarcity. The fear that everyone else is gaining faster. That you're missing out. That you'll never catch up. This isn't just a behavioural glitch—it's a mindset deeply embedded in modern digital finance. But what if that mindset is doing more damage than any bear market ever could? *Scarcity isn't just about having less—it's about believing that less is all there ever will be.* And unless it is named and dismantled, it becomes the operating system for every financial decision that follows.

Scarcity-thinking thrives in environments of speed and spectacle. Crypto is optimised for both. Every week brings new tokens, new narratives, new protocols, each framed as the next frontier. The signals are relentless: "You're early—if you act now." "The window is closing." "Don't be the one who missed the next Ethereum." And so, participation morphs into performance. The market stops being a platform for deliberate strategy and becomes a battleground of reflexes. Scarcity thrives here because it's never truly about assets. It's about *status*. The fear isn't just missing a trade—it's missing a transformation. Missing identity, community, upward mobility.

This emotional infrastructure isn't exclusive to crypto. It's endemic to late capitalism. But decentralised systems amplify it in new ways. In traditional finance, constraints like regulation, institutional gatekeeping, or logistical friction act as behavioural guardrails. Crypto removes those. It grants total autonomy 24/7 access, global liquidity, pseudonymous identity. But without an internal compass, autonomy turns to anxiety. *The freedom to act becomes the compulsion to act.* Scarcity-thinking, unexamined, makes every opportunity feel like a threat: either you grab it or someone else will. Either you win or you fall behind. It's zero-sum logic wrapped in decentralised packaging.

Sufficiency, by contrast, is harder to market—but infinitely more durable. It starts not with a number in an account, but with a framework in the mind. Sufficiency asks: "What is enough, for me, at this stage, given my goals?" It reframes wealth not as an abstract ceiling, but as a contextual threshold. And because it's self-authored, it becomes psychologically stabilising. Sufficiency is not complacency. It's clarity. It doesn't preclude ambition—it calibrates it. *It filters out noise by anchoring the self to values rather than volatility.*

We can see this play out in different kinds of investor behaviour. The scarcity-driven investor chases narratives reactively. They feel anxious when others post screenshots of 10x returns. They constantly reallocate, not because of research, but because of envy. Their sense of progress is externalised. The sufficiency-oriented investor, however, builds with intention. They benchmark against their own needs. They use tools like crypto journals to track not just outcomes, but thought processes. They deploy capital not to signal status but to align with strategy. *They trade less—but grow more.*

One of the most insidious dynamics of scarcity is that it masquerades as urgency. It tells you that waiting is weakness. That caution is cowardice. But often, in decentralised finance, the best decisions are the quiet ones. Saying no to a hyped token. Withdrawing from a yield farm that feels unsustainable. Ignoring a pump driven by celebrity endorsements. These actions don't trend on social media—but they build resilience. Sufficiency equips the investor to weather cycles because it teaches detachment from hype. And detachment, in a permissionless system, is an unspoken superpower.

There is also a moral dimension here. Scarcity-thinking narrows ethical bandwidth. When survival feels at stake, people justify anything—front-running, insider leaks, manipulative influence. They rationalise: "If I don't do it, someone else will." But sufficiency broadens the lens. It allows room for integrity because it isn't driven by panic. It invites long-term thinking, community-building, protocol stewardship. It's not just personally beneficial—it's *collectively vital.* An ecosystem dominated by scarcity-thinking becomes predatory. One shaped by sufficiency can mature with cohesion.

This contrast is especially visible during bear markets. When prices collapse, scarcity-driven individuals spiral. They interpret drawdowns as personal failure. They overtrade. They capitulate.

Those anchored in sufficiency experience discomfort, but not identity crisis. Their worldview wasn't predicated on constant gain. They revisit fundamentals, rebalance calmly, and often position more effectively for the next cycle. *Sufficiency provides a frame of emotional durability.* Not as a passive optimism—but as an active resistance to hysteria.

One might ask: how does one cultivate sufficiency in a world engineered for scarcity? The answer begins with awareness. Naming the mindset is the first step. Recognise the moments when fear—not strategy—is driving action. Then, introduce intentional practices. Regularly define and redefine your personal version of "enough." Set portfolio goals that reflect life priorities, not just market predictions. Use journaling to track emotional patterns around investments. Build routines that prioritise learning and reflection over constant engagement. And importantly, *surround yourself with signals that reinforce sufficiency.* Curate who you follow. Question every claim of easy wealth. Prioritise depth over speed in how you consume information.

Real sufficiency also requires stepping outside of purely financial measures. Crypto promises liberation—but liberation from what? If all it delivers is higher returns but lower peace, then it has failed its human potential. Sufficiency reframes wealth as multidimensional: time, autonomy, relationships, creative freedom. Ask: are your crypto gains expanding these areas? Or are they consuming them? Sufficiency is not just about portfolio management—it's about *life architecture.* It asks whether your systems serve your sovereignty—or just your ego.

There's a deeper philosophical challenge here too. Scarcity-thinking implies that the world is not only finite, but adversarial. That your win necessitates someone else's loss. Sufficiency operates on different assumptions: that value can be created collaboratively; that progress can be distributed; that wealth is not a limited pie but a series of levers—economic, social, technological—that can be pulled for broader benefit. Crypto at its best embodies this logic. Open-source code, decentralised infrastructure, DAOs—all are tools for shared creation. But if we approach them through a scarcity lens, we replicate the very inequalities we sought to disrupt.

The irony is that scarcity-thinking, when left unchecked, leads to precisely what it fears: instability, exhaustion, burnout, regret. It's self-defeating. Sufficiency, meanwhile, creates spaciousness. It leaves room for discernment, ethics, vision. It allows you to be in the market without being consumed by it. And perhaps most importantly, *it teaches you to exit the game at a time of your choosing—not when the game decides for you.*

In the end, this is less about finance than it is about identity. Do you see yourself as someone always one step behind, needing more to feel secure? Or do you see yourself as already equipped, already capable, building from a place of grounded adequacy? Your answer will shape not just your returns—but your experience of life in the decentralised age. Scarcity is a lens. So is sufficiency. One narrows your world. The other opens it. Choose carefully.

Designing a Post-Wealth Life:

What happens when the financial game is over—not because it's lost, but because you've won? It's a question few prepare for and even fewer answer with clarity. Modern wealth culture is built on optimisation, accumulation, and constant motion. But eventually, if systems work and strategies succeed, a threshold is crossed. Money stops being the primary constraint. At that point, most people are left directionless, not liberated. Because despite decades of chasing "freedom," many never learned how to live freely. *Designing a post-wealth life is not about retirement—it's about realignment.* And it begins not with numbers, but with imagination.

This is not a theoretical exercise. The decentralised economy has accelerated wealth creation in ways that outpace traditional timelines. It's no longer rare to see people in their twenties or thirties quietly holding life-changing portfolios. Some sold JPEGs at the right time. Others staked early in DeFi protocols. A few minted the right memecoin or flipped the right NFT. And many, ironically, are still working jobs they no longer need—out of habit, fear, or lack of a compelling alternative. *Wealth without purpose does not breed freedom. It breeds inertia disguised as productivity.*

To design a post-wealth life, one must first reckon with a core truth: money solves money problems. It does not solve identity, relationships, time, or meaning. These are domains that demand conscious authorship. But most people outsource them—letting routines, markets, and social scripts do the designing. When the financial imperative recedes, this outsourcing becomes obvious. Days stretch, not with opportunity, but with emptiness. The challenge shifts from making a living to making a life. And that's a harder game—because there's no ticker, no leaderboard, no metrics.

The shift begins with an uncomfortable question: *If income were permanently removed from the equation, what would you still do?* Strip away obligation, status signalling, and legacy metrics. What remains? Few people can answer that with precision. Even fewer can live it. That's because our economic system conditions us to equate busyness with value and output with worth. Post-wealth life demands a reversal. It's a space where being matters more than doing—and internal alignment replaces external validation.

This doesn't mean withdrawing from ambition. It means *redirecting ambition*. A post-wealth orientation is not passive. It is focused—but differently. It centres around projects, relationships, or missions that are meaningful even without monetisation. It could mean mentoring younger builders in Web3. Funding open-source tools that improve the crypto commons. Writing, teaching, creating art. Raising a family with presence. Building a regenerative farm. None of these require market returns—but all generate value, in the truest sense.

Consider the example of early Ethereum developers who, after realising substantial gains, didn't pivot to consumption—they pivoted to stewardship. They invested time in DAO governance, security research, and ecosystem resilience. Not because they had to, but because they saw meaning in the work itself. Or think of investors who use their post-wealth phase to launch grant programmes, support public goods, or fund privacy tech. Their wealth acts as leverage for intentional impact—not personal expansion.

Designing a post-wealth life also requires *emotional clarity*. Many discover that once survival pressure lifts, suppressed anxieties rise.

Identity was tethered to hustle. Relationships were shaped by scarcity logic. Even relaxation feels unfamiliar. This is where inner work becomes essential. Practices like meditation, somatic therapy, or long-form journaling aren't luxuries—they're navigational tools. Because when you remove money as a compass, you must replace it with something deeper: values, attention, presence.

Another essential lens is *time design*. Post-wealth individuals often find themselves with vast temporal autonomy—and little training in how to use it. The traditional workweek dissolves. But without scaffolding, the days blur. Systems help. Not rigid schedules, but intentional rituals: blocks for deep reading, creative output, exercise, community connection. These create rhythm. They make space sacred. Because ultimately, *how you use your time is the clearest reflection of what you truly value*—not what you say, but what you live.

There's also the matter of social calibration. Post-wealth life can be isolating. Most cultures still equate worth with economic production. Conversations revolve around careers, upgrades, and "what's next." Choosing to step off that axis can feel alienating. That's why community is critical—not one based on shared assets, but shared ethos. People who care less about your balance sheet and more about your alignment. Finding or building that tribe is a project worth prioritising. Because no post-wealth design is complete without relational depth.

Of course, there are dangers. Stagnation. Hedonism. Overengineering. The false belief that one perfect life design will last forever. It won't. Post-wealth life is iterative. It requires periodic reflection and reconfiguration. Desires evolve. Capacities shift. Contexts change. The design is not a blueprint—it's a living framework. What matters is that it is authored—not inherited, not imposed, not automated.

There is a useful mental model borrowed from Stoic philosophy: *live as though you have died and been given your life back*. In this frame, every hour is surplus. Every day is a bonus level. Scarcity vanishes. Gratitude expands. From this posture, one stops trying to optimise life—and begins to *inhabit it.* Fully. Presently. Post-wealth life becomes not a retreat from the world, but a deepening into it.

This is, in a sense, the ultimate test of sovereignty. Crypto promised financial self-sovereignty. But what about existential sovereignty? What about the ability to construct a meaningful life independent of external rewards? Wealth buys optionality. But optionality without intentionality leads to distraction. The highest form of sovereignty is not choosing among dozens of appealing options. It's choosing *deliberately*, with awareness, toward something larger than oneself.

Some may find their post-wealth lives look remarkably like their pre-wealth ones—but with more depth, less urgency. Others will pivot entirely: from engineer to educator, from trader to builder, from founder to philosopher. There's no singular path. What matters is that it is chosen, not drifted into. The tragedy is not in choosing wrong. It is in never choosing at all—letting habit, expectation, or cultural inertia dictate the arc of your life.

Designing a post-wealth life is not the end of the financial conversation. It is the beginning of the philosophical one. It's the point at which money stops being the central narrative—and becomes a supporting character. It's when the spotlight moves to character, integrity, curiosity, contribution. And it's where wealth, finally, is measured not by what is gained—but by *what is sustained, shared, and made meaningful.*

Ask yourself now: if everything you ever needed was already secured, what would you wake up to create? Not to prove. Not to protect. But to honour the one resource that no market can ever inflate—your finite, precious time.

Conclusion
The Invisible Ledger

There exists a ledger the blockchain will never touch. It records no balances, confirms no transfers, signs no blocks into permanence. Yet it's there, quietly inscribed in moments when no one is watching—in the values that seep into code, in the culture shaped by communities, in the contracts we choose to honour or bend. It is the measure between what can be done and what we elect to do. Call it ethical, psychological, personal—this ledger does not chart assets so much as it reveals our orientation to wealth itself. And when the markets cool, the hype dissolves, and the tokens disappear into history, it is often the only account still worth reading.

Crypto, for all its engineering brilliance, has delivered more than a new kind of financial plumbing. It has opened an entirely new philosophical frontier. It invites a decentralised sort of self-inquiry: what becomes of human behaviour when permission is no longer required? What emerges when we trade without intermediaries, speculate without boundaries, and build without gatekeepers? The answers, predictably, are not purely technological—they are deeply human. Decentralisation doesn't abolish power; it shifts its coordinates. And with that shift comes moral volatility, intellectual unease, and, for those willing, astonishing creative scope.

Across these pages we've examined wallets and protocols, wealth strategies and behavioural patterns. But underneath all that detail, one question has been quietly pressing: what sort of person are you becoming in this space? Not merely how much you've made, but how you think now. What you prize. Whom you trust. What compromises you accept. And perhaps most telling, what you're teaching others—deliberately or by osmosis.

This is the invisible ledger. It keeps no public hash, yet it tracks the architecture of your judgement: your focus, your decision frameworks, your willingness to wait, to resist the frenzy, to think with rigour, to act with principle. It's written in the choice to front-run a trade or strengthen a market's integrity; to back public goods or chase private windfalls; to share insight or hoard advantage. It's reflected in your handling of volatility, your posture toward loss, your definition of success.

To engage with crypto in any sustained way without recognising this dimension is to miss half the picture. The novelty will fade. Yields will shrink. The thrill will fracture. Then you are left facing questions few investors expect: and now? Was it worth the hours, the risk, the faith? What, besides a balance sheet, did I build? What did I learn about myself in the absence of a central bank's oversight? These aren't sentimental diversions; they cut to the structural heart of your legacy.

Think of the DAO contributor whose name never appeared, yet whose work was meticulous and transparent. Or the validator who reported a vulnerability rather than exploit it. Or the anonymous educator posting clear, measured threads for understanding's sake, not for followers. None of them headline rich lists, yet their choices accrue a different kind of yield—reputation, trust, cultural capital. Assets that don't chart on CoinGecko but sustain ecosystems long after bull runs end.

And then there are those who gamed loopholes, manipulated governance, engineered exit scams dressed as breakthroughs. Profitable, for a season. But in doing so they impoverished trust—the bloodstream of any decentralised system. Without trust, a protocol degenerates into a casino, collaboration collapses into transaction, innovation sinks into opportunism. The invisible ledger tallies not in numbers, but in direction: entropy or coherence?

Here's why this matters more in crypto than in traditional finance. In the old system, ethics are often externalised—compliance departments, regulatory bodies, formal enforcement. In decentralised finance, the referee is mostly gone. Responsibility migrates inward. Fewer rules mean more is left to character. The constraints loosen; integrity must be self-supplied. That's not just a challenge—it's a rare opportunity. Because while crypto is indeed testing new architectures for money, it is also testing new architectures for trust, governance, and collaboration. And here, code may set the parameters, but conduct determines the outcome.

To be clear, this is not an appeal to romanticise the space. If anything, it's the opposite. The nastiest bugs aren't always in smart contracts; they hide in human incentives, blind spots, and tribal echo chambers. The invisible ledger catches these distortions early. When you're tempted by a story you privately doubt. When you excuse an action because "everyone else is doing it." When you chase optics instead of outcomes. These moments aren't isolated—they're cultural signals. Ignore them, and they set the tone.

Which is why self-reflection is not ornamental here; it is a form of governance. Not for the protocol, but for yourself. Write things down. Ask uncomfortable questions. Revisit old decisions. Listen for dissonance. Seek the friction in your own logic. These aren't just exercises in personal growth—they are political acts in a system where moral direction emerges from the sum of countless individual choices. The healthiest decentralised futures will be cultivated as much in conscience as in code.

So perhaps wealth, in this realm, is better understood not simply as a stack of tokens, but as the accumulated proof of choices made consistently over time. Choices that both reveal and reinforce what you value. Each trade, a kind of vote. Each contract, a statement. Each transaction, a fresh entry in that invisible ledger.

If that sounds philosophical, it's because it is. Crypto is more than a financial instrument—it's a mirror, a provocateur, a stress test for your beliefs about autonomy, fairness, participation, and potential. And just as markets cycle through phases, so does one's relationship to the space: the rush of novelty, the drift toward scepticism, the settling into clarity. Some depart. Some double down. A few step back far enough to ask not only how to win, but why to play at all.

This closing chapter is not an epilogue—it's an opening. An invitation to inspect the patterns beneath your portfolio. To audit intentions with the same care as holdings. To measure success not in exits alone, but in contributions—to people, to protocols, to principles. To see value not just in what you take out, but in what remains because you were here.

For long after charts collapse and headlines fade, the invisible ledger endures. And it will ask, as it asks all of us: What did you build that others can trust? What did you learn that others can use? What example did you leave that others might follow? These are not rhetorical flourishes; they are architectural blueprints. Because the future of decentralised wealth will be written not only in code, capital, or computation, but in character.

The final chapter invites readers to reflect on the non-monetary gains they've accrued:

There's a kind of wealth no protocol can mint, no market can measure, and no wallet can hold. It doesn't fluctuate with the charts, and it cannot be lost in a liquidation cascade. It is the wealth of *clarity*—knowing why you act. The wealth of *calm*—remaining anchored in volatility. The wealth of *conviction*—persisting with integrity in a world wired for distraction. This closing reflection is not about finalising a strategy, but about *activating a stance.* It invites you not to chase more, but to *stand for more*—to exit the book not merely as a better investor, but as a more intentional designer of the values you believe wealth should reflect.

Crypto may have drawn you in through returns, but what it leaves you with—if you've paid attention—is a deeper interrogation of *what returns are worth chasing at all.* It's easy to see DeFi as a set of mechanisms for yield. Harder, but far more essential, is to see it as a proving ground for *discipline, discernment, and design.* Most people come to the space for upside. Some stay for autonomy. But only a few come to understand its deeper potential: as a canvas for *reimagining what human systems can incentivise when trust is built into the substrate.*

Let's be honest. Along the way, you've likely experienced FOMO, made suboptimal trades, second-guessed decisions, reacted to narratives. Everyone does. But what matters more than any individual trade is whether your *thinking has changed.* Whether you've developed the ability to see hype cycles for what they are, to separate signal from noise, and to regulate yourself in systems where no one else will. *This book has not asked you to predict the next bull market. It has asked you to become the kind of person who doesn't need one to feel successful.*

If you've taken that seriously, you've started accumulating something rarer than tokens: mental liquidity. The capacity to shift perspectives without abandoning principles. To hold ideas loosely, but values tightly. To move between optimism and scepticism without becoming cynical. To understand that wealth is not defined by how much you hold, but by how little it takes to disturb your peace.

Clarity is underrated in financial thinking. We are conditioned to seek complexity, to believe more data equals better decisions. But clarity is subtraction, not addition. It is the discipline of reducing decisions to their essentials. Of knowing *your* why in a sea of conflicting signals. And clarity often emerges not in bull runs, but in collapses—when illusions fall away, and only the necessary remains. To leave this book with clarity is to have gained something irreversible.

Calm, too, is a form of mastery. Crypto trains volatility into your nervous system if you let it. But volatility is not just a market condition—it's a *test of character.* Remaining calm when the floor disappears is not about detachment from outcomes. It's about *alignment with process.* When you've built your system around principles, not prices, you don't need perfect information to act—you need poise. And that poise becomes your edge. Not flashy, not Twitter-viral, but quietly compounding.

Conviction, finally, is what allows you to act decisively—not impulsively—in a decentralised world. There is no boss to check your reasoning. No regulator to validate your ethics. Conviction is what you rely on when due diligence meets uncertainty. It's what turns information into intelligence. More importantly, it's what turns speculation into stewardship. *When you operate with conviction, you stop reacting and start architecting.*

But this chapter does not only look backwards. It calls you forward. To ask: now that you've learned how crypto works—*what will you make it mean?* Wealth, if it is to be more than accumulation, must become articulation. A way of expressing your commitments in capital form. If you've automated your strategies, documented your thinking, resisted the shiny objects, and defined your post-wealth life, then this final question matters: *What values will your gains fund?*

You can continue to speculate. You can optimise for yield. But you can also begin to *construct new value systems*, using the same composability crypto enables for code. What does it mean to *embed your ethics into your allocations?* To *support networks that align with your view of a healthier internet, a more participatory economy, a more human-centred protocol stack?* The tools exist. The clarity now does too. What's left is the will to deploy—not just capital, but conscience.

And here lies the most radical proposition this book makes: that you don't just have a portfolio—you have *power*. Not the institutional kind. Not the political kind. But the power to shape emerging systems by what you choose to learn, build, fund, and support. Crypto collapses the distinction between participant and architect. Every action is a vote. Every allocation is a signal. Every contract is a culture-shaping artefact. *You're no longer just investing in assets—you're expressing belief through structure.*

So what are you building? What will remain when your charts are silent, your keys inactive, and your dashboards unread? Will you have produced only returns—or results? Only profits—or *principles*? Will others be better off because you were in this space—not just financially, but in how they think, decide, and navigate their own invisible ledgers? These are not philosophical musings. They are practical questions for a decentralised world where *impact is the only real legacy*.

Many people will close a book like this and ask, "What next?" The honest answer is: nothing changes—unless *you* do. Unless you continue to question convenience, examine incentives, resist noise, and embody the values you've claimed to learn. You are not waiting for the next protocol to launch. You are not holding your breath for the next market cycle. *You are already in motion—as a system-building organism*. You have agency. And now, you have frameworks. Use them.

What crypto needed at first was liquidity. What it needs now is *leadership*. Not from figureheads or influencers, but from those who quietly build ethical systems, who model sustainable wealth, who create without exploiting, and who teach without condescension.

The kind of leadership that doesn't signal virtue, but *embodies it*—because it's inseparable from how one moves through the world.

So as the last word on the last page, let this be a challenge disguised as closure: don't just chase wealth—*embody it.* Be the person who makes others feel that abundance is possible without extraction, that excellence need not come at the cost of ethics, that wealth can be a reflection of wholeness, not a replacement for it. That in building new systems, we might rediscover older truths: that what you hold is never more important than what you *honour.*

About the Author

Julien Ashcroft is a financial futurist and behavioural strategist who bridges the gap between emerging technologies and timeless investment principles. With a background in economics, digital finance, and human psychology, Julien has spent over a decade studying how individuals relate to money in an increasingly decentralised world. His work dissects the emotional, philosophical, and technological dimensions of wealth in the digital age. Known for his clarity, depth, and contrarian wisdom, Julien empowers readers to build financial conviction in a landscape defined by hype and volatility. From Wallet to Wealth is the result of years spent guiding investors, thinkers, and curious sceptics toward a more mindful, long-term approach to crypto and value creation.

www.ingramcontent.com/pod-product-compliance
Lightning Source LLC
Chambersburg PA
CBHW031345230926
51848CB00002B/387
9789371770583